PRAISE FOR:

From Ruins to Restoration

"*From Ruins to Restoration* is a powerful reminder that God does some of His greatest work in the rubble of our lives. As a minister and a retired Chief Warrant Officer who has walked with men and women through some of their hardest battles, I know the importance of hope, healing, and spiritual renewal. These devotions speak directly to weary hearts, pointing them toward the One who restores, rebuilds, and breathes life into broken places. This book is more than a devotional—it's a lifeline for anyone longing to encounter God's restoring grace."
—Anthony Hayes, Ordained Minister & CW4 (Ret.), United States Army

"This devotional collection is a refreshing well for the believer who feels dry, stuck, or overwhelmed by life's trials. *From Ruins to Restoration* takes readers on a journey through Scripture, story, and reflection, offering a gentle yet powerful call back to the heart of God. Each devotion carries the voice of experience and the anointing of the Holy Spirit. Whether you are a new believer or a seasoned follower of Christ, this book will strengthen your walk and remind you that God is still in the restoration business."
—David Rodriguez, Pastor & Evangelist

"*From Ruins to Restoration* is a beautifully woven tapestry of truth, transparency, and spiritual insight. As someone who has written about the complexities of human emotion and the tender work of healing, I deeply appreciate the authenticity and compassion these devotions offer. Each page invites readers to slow down, breathe, and rediscover the restorative presence of God in everyday life. This devotional is a gift to anyone searching for hope and a reminder that restoration is always possible."
—Gwendolyn Odom, University Professor & Award-Winning Author of *You Don't Know Just How I Feel*

From Ruins to Restoration

50 Devotions to Revive Your Spirit and Renew Your Faith

Compiled and edited by: Dr. Katherine Hutchinson-Hayes
Assistant Editor: Crystal Johnson

Unless otherwise noted, Scripture quotations used in this book are from *The Holy Bible*, New International Version (NIV). © 1973, 1978, 1984, 2011 International Bible Society. Used by permission of Zondervan Bible Publishers.

Other Scripture references are from the following sources:
King James Version (KJV)
New King James Version (NKJV), ©1979, 1980, 1982, Thomas Nelson, Inc.
English Standard Version® (ESV) © 2001 by Crossway, a publishing ministry of Good News Publishers
New American Standard (NAS), Copyright © 1960, 1962, 1963, 1968, 1971, 1972, 1973, 1975, 1977, 1995 by THE LOCKMAN FOUNDATION
New Living Translation (NLT), copyright ©1996, 2004, 2015 by Tyndale House Foundation. Used by permission of Tyndale House Publishers, Carol Stream, Illinois 60188. All rights reserved.

Copyright © 2025 Dr. Katherine Hutchinson-Hayes. All rights reserved.
ISBN: 978-1-970354-03-4
E-book ISBN: 978-1-970354-04-1
LCCN: 2025924936

Publisher: Dressed in Love Press, LLC
www.drkatherinehayes.com

Cover Designer: Dr. Katherine Hutchinson-Hayes
Assistant Editor: Crystal Johnson
Book Interior Designer: Jenifer Jennings

First Edition
Printed in the United States of America

Table of Contents

FOREWORD

HGTV is stuffed with restoration projects, not new builds. Why? Because restorations are usually DIY projects, and professionals handle new construction. We're DIY people. We watch and imagine turning broken into whole and ugly into beautiful.

Though we may fail at remodeling that mustard-tiled vintage half bath, we're capable of transformative restoration in spaces that matter most.

Biblical restoration requires both DIY and expert intervention. We get to do our part. God must do his.

And the "spaces" to be restored?

They're far more complex—and far more rewarding—than most fixer-uppers. The primary projects are ourselves, others, relationships, and the entire universe. So, grab a hammer and a hat, and prepare for action. When we do our part, God does his. I've seen him in action.

I used to manage my anger by fighting, sometimes physically, and often verbally. I recall a day when I stayed at the table during a challenging conversation and, without thinking, kept my emotions in check. No one was more surprised than I.

On the drive home, as silly as this is, I did a happy dance in the car. I looked in the rearview mirror and said, "Look at you. You're growing."

It was worth celebrating because I'd worked hard at transforming my character. But I didn't do it alone. I had a mentor who led me to train with God in intentional ways. And God did it. He restored me a little closer to who he always intended me to be. That deserved a dance.

This book provides daily devotions to help you ponder, plan, and play your part in God's massive restoration project. Each writer will challenge and comfort you. They'll connect you to the big story that began in Eden and won't end until Jesus returns to "restore all things" (Acts 1:6).

Jesus's disciples asked him if he was ready to restore everything as he was about to ascend back into heaven. He said something like, "That's none of your business," and then, in Acts 1:8, he focused them on their business.

He instructed them to spend their time proclaiming the good news and bringing the Kingdom. In other words, start restoring.

In the Old and New Testaments, the ancient words translated "restore" or "restoration" mean to heal, make whole, put in order, or rebuild for the original purpose.

We have the privilege of joining God to:
- Make whole those wrestling with all types of sin and wounds, including ourselves.
- Put in order—relationships with people we've hurt—or who've disappointed us.
- Pray for physical healing.
- Invite others to spiritual salvation.
- Rebuild society for its original purpose—through politics, business, art, education, church, medicine, the gospel, and every creative outlet God inspires.

Let the restoration stories within these devotions bring a smile to your face—just like the big reveal on your favorite makeover show. Revel in God's transformations. Do a happy dance.

But mostly, listen deeply for blueprints on the challenges around you. Then, take Your Turn, and find someone—or something—to restore to breathtaking beauty.

—Rodney Combs, Ph.D. Author, Speaker, Personal and Professional Coach

Katherine Hutchinson-Hayes
Clear Vision:
For Seeing Our Way To Success

Where there is no vision, the people perish: but he
that keepeth the law, happy is he.
Proverbs 29:18 (KJV)

As a new year unfolds, many may feel the call to set objectives in their spiritual lives, whether new in faith or seasoned believers. Our walk with Christ also has a practical aspect, which requires us to be mindful of how we present ourselves to the world. To grow in our relationship with God, we may need to refine our spiritual disciplines, enhance our engagement in our communities, attend church events to network with fellow believers and stay informed about the teachings and trends in our faith.

Empowering Others Through Purposeful Faith and Service

We can inspire and uplift those around us through our actions and words, providing encouragement and hope. However, achieving this requires more than mere desire; it demands a clear understanding of our purpose and a well-defined plan. This includes identifying our community, building our faith-based brand, engaging with others through love and service, and continually growing our knowledge of God's Word. By seeking guidance and staying committed, we can achieve great things for His Kingdom and positively impact the lives of those we encounter.

Aligning Goals with Christian Values for Spiritual Growth

Setting goals is a vital aspect of our journey as followers of Christ. It helps us stay focused, motivated, and accountable for our growth. As explained in Proverbs 29:18, we fail when we neglect to plan. By aligning our objectives with our Christian values, we can ensure our efforts are directed toward what truly matters.

Here are some tips to keep in mind while creating goals that align with our faith:

1. **Seek guidance:** It is essential to start with a firm foundation in Christ. Seeking advice from mentors and seasoned Christians can provide valuable insights and inspiration. Before embarking on new endeavors, let us reach out to those with more experience in faith and ask for their wisdom to guide us forward.

2. **Establish a clear vision:** Define your goals in your spiritual journey. Write specific, measurable, achievable objectives to gain a comprehensive understanding of your aspirations. This clarity can motivate you and help you track your progress, increasing your chances of success.

3. **Align goals with your values:** To effectively share Christ's love, our goals must reflect our beliefs in Him. Reflect on your faith and ensure your aspirations align with your values. This way, you can create a life that truly resonates with your calling and positively impacts your world.

4. **Break down goals into smaller steps:** When we set significant aspirations, it's easy to feel overwhelmed. We can make them more achievable by breaking them down into smaller, manageable steps. Map out a plan with specific actions that will propel you toward your goals. This approach will help you feel more in control of your growth and encourage you to keep going, even when faced with challenges.

5. **Hold yourself accountable:** To fulfill our commitments, we must set objectives and hold ourselves accountable. Scheduling regular check-ins with ourselves and trusted members of our community can help us evaluate our progress and determine whether we're on track. This practice can help us identify areas that need adjustment or where additional effort is required.

6. **Celebrate your success:** Acknowledge small victories, as they reinforce positive behavior and maintain motivation. Learn from setbacks by reflecting on what went wrong and using that knowledge to improve your approach. Embracing a growth mindset will allow you to view challenges as opportunities for spiritual growth.

Empowering Change Through Faith and Action

As followers of Christ, we can accomplish incredible things and impact the world through our faith and actions. By setting goals and dedicating ourselves wholeheartedly to our spiritual journey, we can make meaningful contributions to our communities. Let's strive with unwavering passion to create lives that inspire, motivate, and transform the hearts of those around us.

Prayer:

Dear Heavenly Father, as we enter this new year, we seek Your guidance and wisdom in creating a vision for success and setting our goals. Help us to align our desires with Your will and empower us to take meaningful steps toward growth in our faith. May our lives reflect Your love and grace, touching the hearts of those around us. Strengthen us in our journey, and let us celebrate the victories and the lessons learned along the way. In Jesus' name, we pray. Amen.

Your Turn:

Take time to reflect on your spiritual goals for this year. What steps can you take to grow closer to God? Consider writing down your aspirations and breaking them into actionable steps. Share these goals with a close friend or mentor for support and accountability. Pray for guidance and strength to navigate your path.

Katherine Hutchinson-Hayes
Double Portion Blessings: Embracing God's Restoration

Instead of your shame, you will receive a double portion, and instead of disgrace, you will rejoice in your inheritance. And so you will inherit a double portion in your land, and everlasting joy will be yours.
Isaiah 61:7 (NIV)

The Story of His Abundant Grace

There was a time in my writing career when I felt undeserving of the opportunities God was placing before me. I questioned whether I was qualified enough, talented enough, or worthy of the blessings He was pouring into my life. Honestly, I sometimes continue to struggle in this area. Yet, in these moments of doubt, God reminds me that He's not limited by my inadequacies—His plans are far greater than any of my many fears.

I remember vividly a season when I was on the verge of giving up, feeling the sting of rejection letters and the weight of imposter syndrome. I even began actively preparing to return to my former occupation of school administration. But God, in His faithfulness, brought renewal into my heart. Doors began to open unexpectedly: invitations to speak, opportunities to publish, and moments where my words resonated deeply with others. It wasn't because of anything I had done but because of His abundant grace.

I realized that this season wasn't about my qualifications—it was about leaning into God's calling for renewal, restoration, and rebirth. And through it all, He gave me a double portion of blessings, just as Isaiah 61:7 promises.

Three Ways God Restores Us

1. **He Renews Our Purpose:** When life feels aimless or stagnant, God breathes new purpose into our lives. His plans are always for our good, and He equips us to walk in them. In my writing journey, He renewed my purpose by reminding me that my words could glorify Him and encourage others.

2. **He Restores Our Confidence:** It's easy to feel disqualified by our past mistakes or failures. But God restores confidence by reminding us that we are His chosen vessels. He does not call the qualified—He qualifies the called.

3. **He Rebirths Our Joy:** When shame and discouragement steal our joy, God replaces it with everlasting joy. His blessings remind us of His faithfulness and goodness, and He fills our hearts with gratitude for His perfect plan.

A Prayer for Renewal and Restoration:

Dear Heavenly Father, Thank You for being a God of rebirth, restoration, and renewal. Even when we feel undeserving, You pour out Your blessings and give us a double portion of joy. Help us to lean into Your promises and trust in Your plans for our lives. Renew our hearts, restore our confidence, and rebirth our joy so we may walk boldly in the purpose You've set before us. In Jesus' name, Amen.

Your Turn:

Have you experienced God's restoration in your life? Take a moment to reflect on areas needing renewal or restoration.

- Write down three areas where you trust God for a double portion of blessings.
- Pray over those areas and ask God for guidance and renewal.
- Share your testimony with someone who needs encouragement today.

Let's walk into this season of renewal together, trusting that His plans are better than anything we could imagine

<u>Andy Hollifield</u>
Restored Beauty:
God's Heart Revealed in the T-Bird Journey

*...For the LORD sees not as man sees; for man
looketh on the outward appearance, but the LORD
looketh on the heart.*
1 Samuel 16:7 (KJV)

Sam Sneed was headed back to his hometown of Springdale. His family moved away when he was a kid, and he'd never returned. Now retired from the military, one of his childhood neighbors, Mrs. Nolan, sent word that she would like him to visit her in the retirement home where she now lived. Her husband, Bernie, had passed away years before Sam retired.

"Sam," Mrs. Nolan said abruptly when he first walked in. "I need a favor."

"Yes, Ma'am, I'll do anything I can to help you. What do you need?"

"I'm an old woman now, and my last wish is to see mine and Bernie's little farm again. Could you oblige me that one request?"

"Sure. I'd be honored to. When would you like to go?"

"I'm ready now, and I've already gotten approval from the staff," she said with a mischievous grin.

"Now is as good a time as any," Sam replied. "I'll go get the car."

"Yes, you will," she told him. He attributed her unusual remark to her age and thought nothing more of it.

When they arrived at the old farm, Mrs. Nolan told Sam to park in front of the barn. Slowly getting out of the car, she looked at him and said, "Follow me."

The spry little old lady moved with a purpose and drive she probably hadn't had in years. The rollers creaked like the train wheels screeching when Sam pushed the barn door open for the first time in years. The barn didn't need much light. Between the windows Mr. Nolan put in when he built it and the sheets of the tin roof that had long since blown away, there was plenty of light.

"Sam, I want you to have everything in this barn if you clean it for me. Sell it, keep it, or whatever. It's yours to do what you want with. There's no telling what antiques and old tools you'll find."

"Mrs. Nolan, I don't know what to say but thank you. Of course, I'll do it for you," Sam replied, completely surprised by her request.

"One more thing. Pull that big tarp back. Do it kind of easy," she said.

Sam slowly pulled it back and stopped suddenly. "You've got to be kidding me. Is that Mr. Bernie's old T-Bird? I haven't seen that since I was a kid. I remember him raising the hood and talking about the 312 Overhead Valve V-8 power plant sitting there like a pearl in an oyster. I didn't know anything he was talking about, but I knew he was proud of it," Sam said. "What am I supposed to do with it?" he asked as he pulled the tarp back and gently wiped some dust from the hood. "It's fire engine red," just like I remembered. She sure is a beauty."

"Do what you want with it, but I hope you'll restore it and drive it. Bernie would've wanted you to have it. He remembered how much you liked it."

"But, I can't accept that. It's too much," Sam protested to no avail.

"Yes, you can. You said you'd help me. No one else could appreciate and love that car like you. Besides, you're a man of your word, and you said you'd clean out everything in the barn," Mrs. Nolan replied, flashing her mischievous grin once more.

As with anything that old, it would require a lot of love and care. Sam realized it would mean a lot of weeknights burning the midnight oil and a lot of weekend plans would be changed. In the end, he knew it would be worth every minute of his time. Since sixth grade, he had loved the '57 T-birds, especially the ragtops, as they were called decades ago. Posters of them had adorned his bedroom walls as a boy and now plastered the walls of his garage.

That's how Christ is with us. He doesn't see us as man does, as described in 1 Samuel 16:7 (KJV). He looks past our outward appearance and at our hearts. He sees us for who we can become through His workmanship, not who we are in our broken and dismantled states. While others would look at Mr. Nolan's old T-Bird as a "dirty bird," Sam acted as God would and saw its full potential. Therefore, that dirty bird was restored to its rightful condition with time, money, and dedication.

Similarly, God takes us, even when we're long forgotten by most, covered with the dust of sin, and pulls away all the layers individually. He gently wipes away the dust, revealing what we could be. He sees the beauty in us that no one else does. He went to Calvary's cross and gave His life so we could be forgiven, restored, and again become useful and shine. Whatever amount of time, cost, and effort it takes to restore us to fellowship with His Father, He considered it worth every minute, not because of what we were, but what we could be with enough of His love and care.

You may think you're so covered with sin and forgotten that you're not worth restoring. Remember, God doesn't look at the outward appearance but at the heart. He breathed the breath of life into you, and you became a living soul. He has invested his time into you, breathed life into you, and gave his Son to die for your sins. He thinks you're worth restoring, just like that dirty bird.

Prayer:

Lord, I pray that someone will read this and realize you see them as worthy, not as they see themselves. As Sam saw the beauty and value of that old, forgotten, dirty T-bird, let them realize that's how you see them: completely worth saving and restoring.

Your turn:

To restore is "the act or process of returning something to its earlier good, position, or owner."[1] We're the gem of God's creation. We're the only creatures God created in His image.

- What specific aspects of your life do you feel God is urging you to return to a state of wholeness or improvement?
- Are there relationships, habits, or dreams that you believe need healing or rejuvenation?

- In what ways do you think restoring these elements could enhance your spiritual journey and overall well-being?
- Have you taken the time to reflect on the signs or messages you may have received regarding these areas of restoration?
- What actionable steps can you take to begin the process of restoration in those areas God is calling you to focus on?

Katherine Hutchinson-Hayes
The Power of Restoration:
A Legacy of Renewal

*And he who was seated on the throne said, "Behold,
I am making all things new." Also he said, "Write this
down, for these words are trustworthy and true."
Revelation 21:5 (ESV)*

In a world that often feels fractured and overwhelming, restoration provides a beacon of hope. The Bible frequently speaks of renewal through personal redemption, the restoration of relationships, or the rejuvenation of our surroundings. Restoration isn't merely about fixing what is broken—it's about bringing new life to what once thrived. One poignant example of this power of restoration comes from my childhood—through my father's hands.

Two years after my parents moved to this country, they purchased their first home. It wasn't fancy. Instead, it was a paint-peeling, dusty-fixer-upper with the floorboards so damaged you could see upstairs from the ground floor. I can vividly remember my father, a natural craftsman, rolling up his sleeves and diving into the project. He transformed that house with remarkable skill, vision, and passion. Walls were painted, floors were refinished, and gardens were cultivated. That house became a testament to his dedication and artistry.

The Visionary Handyman: Restoring Homes and Hearts in the Community

But my father's restoration work did not stop with our home. He began using his skills to help others in our community. Neighbors would call him for advice or assistance. What started as helping friends spiraled into a small business where he would rehab broken-down places. People would come to admire the beautiful churches, businesses, and homes he renovated and the spirit of hope and community he fostered. He became known as a modern visionary, not just a handyman, but the owner of his construction company—restoring buildings and the hearts of those living there.

This legacy of restoration deeply impacted my siblings and me. Growing up, we witnessed the transformative power of hard work and dedication. My father showed us that restoration goes beyond the physical—it transcends into relationships, community ties, and personal growth. Each of us was inspired to view challenges as opportunities for renewal. Whether assisting him on a project or bringing a friend in need to our home, we learned that restoration was about love, service, and the willingness to invest time and resources into something greater than ourselves.

The Divine Power of Restoration: Becoming New Creations Through Grace

The word says, "Behold, I am making all things new." Also he said, "Write this down, for these words are trustworthy and true" (Revelation 21:5 ESV). As we reflect on the power of restoration in our lives, we should acknowledge the ultimate restorer—God. Just as my father transformed homes, God transforms our hearts and lives. The old may pass away, but we become new creations through His grace. The scars we bear do not define us; instead, they remind us of His unfailing love and the journey He has taken us on.

A Prayer for Restoration:

Heavenly Father, we come before You, grateful for the work of restoration you perform in our lives. Thank you for the examples set before us and for the opportunities to heal and renew. Help us see the broken places in our lives and our communities—may Your Spirit guide our hands and hearts as we seek to restore our surroundings and the relationships that matter. Give us the courage to step out in faith and be agents of change, mirroring the restoration that You exemplify through Your love. In Jesus' name, we pray, Amen.

Your Turn:

Now, I invite you to reflect on the power of restoration in your own life. Think of spaces, relationships, or personal struggles that might need a little TLC. Challenge yourself to take a step toward restoring something this week. Whether that means volunteering to help someone with home repairs, reaching out to mend a broken relationship, or even taking time for personal growth, embrace the spirit of restoration.

Let's cultivate communities of hope, like my dad did, and remember that, through God's grace, we can all be instruments of renewal. What will you restore today?

Kathy Keenum
Do You Want An Abundant Harvest?

*"I will repay you for the years that the swarming
locust ate, the young locust, the destroying locust, and
the devouring locust—My great army that I sent
against you. You will have plenty to eat and be
satisfied. You will praise the name of Yahweh your
God, who has dealt wondrously with you. My people
will never again be put to shame."*
Joel 2:25-26 (HCSB)

Each day, the sun rises, dispelling the darkness of night. During these seasons, we often confront loss, anxiety, and worry. The devastation is vast. These burdens wear down our humanity until we are hardly the people we once were. Our lives can become wastelands of regret and hardship. Yet, the Lord transforms that wasteland into a beautiful, complete, thriving garden with a bountiful harvest.

The passage in Joel 2:25-26 called for the people of Israel to turn away from spiritual complacency and turn to the Lord in worship. The Lord's army (locusts) caused great anguish. Then, in compassion, His promises brought about a great harvest, healing the land and hearts of those who'd lost so much.

Joel explains that God is in the business of redeeming and restoring. Israel suffered greatly as cicadae destroyed their crops, fields, and land. Drought filled the land, and the people suffered. In Joel 2:26, God promises restoration and abundant blessings. The harvest will be full, and blessings will abound. God is always faithful to his word. As the people recovered from their hardship, they were blessed with abundant food, prosperity, and joy.

Restoring Our Relationship with the Lord Through All Seasons

When dark, barren wasteland experiences overwhelm us, the Lord is there, just as He was for His people in the Bible.

Additionally, there are things we should do to benefit from the rich promises in God's scripture from which we may continually draw. We can:

1. **Restore**—our relationship with the Lord. Draw close during times of desolation and times of plenty. Praise Him during all the seasons, up and down, good and bad, light and dark. As He restored the land after the locust, He will restore us after times of trouble.

2. **Renew**—our daily walk with Him. Renew our walk of faith. A transformation from what was to what is. When we let God work in and on us, His transformations always result in something greater than we originally had in mind.

3. **Hope**—in God's promise of abundance. Israel suffered during the locust invasion. The pests ate everything, destroying crops and plants. However, God blessed his people after this, bringing promise, hope, and abundance after trial and hardship. This same promise of abundant hope is available to us.

Prayer:

Lord, Thank you for your promises of abundance, prosperity, and joy. Please be with us during trials. Restore and strengthen our faith as we draw closer to you. Bless us that our focus will remain on you during times of loss and renew our joy as we walk the path you have for us. Amen.

Your Turn:

- Have you ever been through trials in your life?
- Did you rely on God and his promises, or did you rely on yourself?
- Which way worked better?

Colleen Howard
Fix Your Eyes

. . .And let us run with perseverance the race marked
out for us, fixing our eyes on Jesus, the pioneer and
perfecter of faith. For the joy set before him he
endured the cross, scorning its shame, and sat down
at the right hand of the throne of God.
Hebrews 12:1-2 (NIV)

I love this scripture reference to Jesus as a pioneer and perfector of faith. According to the Dictionary, a pioneer is a "person, group, or thing that is first or among the earliest in any field of inquiry, enterprise, or development - first to enter or settle a region." Jesus paved the way for us to know God. He is the way, the truth, and the life. We cannot go to the Father except through Jesus Christ.

Why do we fix our eyes on Jesus? He is our redeemer. He loves us and equips us. But how can we focus on Him with many demands and people competing for our attention? How do we make Jesus the focus of our daily lives?

As I pondered these questions, I was reminded of my childhood ballet lessons. I adored attending classes and taking lessons twice a week through elementary school and junior high. But when I started high school, I was ready for something new and switched to modern dance. My years of ballet were an excellent foundation for moving into the contemporary dance arena. There are many dance genres, but in almost every type of dance, there comes a time when the awe-inspiring spin takes center stage, and the audience is mesmerized by the dancer's speed and precision.

Picture a ballerina executing a complete turn, spinning on her toes. She moves incredibly fast and then abruptly stops without losing her focus or balance. How does she do that?

It's a technique called spotting. The dancer selects an object at eye level as her focal point. As her body spins, she keeps her eyes on that spot. Then, she quickly whips her head around to maintain her focus. It's a fast response. It's flawless and beautiful. This move is a pirouette.

However, if the ballerina diverts her eyes from the focal point, she will lose her balance and tumble to the stage floor.

For those who follow Jesus Christ, He is our only focal point. What happens if we take our eyes off Him? Our vision blurs, and before we know it, we tumble to the ground just like the ballerina. Sometimes, when we're off course, we are aware of the misstep immediately; other times, it takes a few days or more to fully accept what has happened. Let the visual image of the dancer be a reminder to zoom in on the Savior.

One thing is certain: when we lose our footing, the Holy Spirit will whisper, saying, "Turn your eyes toward Jesus. He will set your feet on solid ground and steady you as you walk." Let's lift our hands to the heavens with shouts of praise and follow Jesus, the powerful pioneer, who made it possible for us to know God.

Prayer:

Dear Jesus, we are thankful beyond measure for the sacrifice you endured on the cross for us. Help us to run the race with perseverance and keep our eyes fixed on You. We trust you to steady our feet and hold us upright. Keep our hearts firmly planted in the Word of God so that we may reflect your light. Thanks be to God, Amen.

Your Turn:

Reflect on a time when your focus on Jesus was blurry.

- What distracted you?
- How did you get back on track and fix your eyes on Him?

Vonyee K. Carrington
One Lemon at a Time:
Transform Your Life!

*I had fainted. Unless I had believed to see the
goodness of the Lord in the land of the living. Wait on
the Lord: Be of good courage, and he will shall
strengthen thine heart: wait, I say, on the LORD.
Psalm 27:13-14 (KJV)*

Have you ever sinned? I am talking about the type of sin in which you deliberately decide, "I am going to do it despite what the Word of God says." I have.

The true anguish and turmoil came after I had carried out the act. I remember questioning myself, "What have I done?" I also have a memory of proclaiming that I belonged to God. However, I now understand I cannot claim to be His—if I willfully sin when I know better. Repeatedly, I asked myself, "What's wrong with me?

Remorse set in. I worried God wouldn't love me. My mind told me, "You'll never see the goodness of the Lord in the land of the living" (Psalm 27:13). Then I thought, "Why even continue to serve God? There is no recovery from this."

I was in one of these mental battles when I went lemon picking recently. I was anxious that God would never forgive me for committing my sin. I kept thinking God would never bless me after this.

Yet, God is merciful.

A friend invited me to pick lemons from a tree, and I wasn't sure what to expect. Upon reaching the location, I gazed at the tree and thought, "How will we get all those lemons down?" I hadn't brought any tools with me. My friend had a short ladder, and another friend who owned the tree gave us a fruit hook. I asked if she had a citrus picker, a basket with prongs on a long pole, and she did.

The citrus picker should have made the job easier. My friend was pulling down four lemons to my one, while I should have been pulling down more. I didn't understand what was wrong. After a few unsuccessful attempts, I looked at the picker. Half of the prongs were mangled, making it difficult to grasp the larger lemons.

I had to figure out how to use the picker to my advantage. Four of the eight prongs weren't damaged. I began angling the picker so that I grasped the fruit. The Lord began to speak to me in that moment of my sin. He asked me, "Did you repent of the sin?" I responded, "Yes. Let me repent again. Lord Jesus, please forgive me." He said, "You are forgiven. That's why Jesus came."

My mind was blown! It was as easy as inviting God to communicate with me so that I could attain forgiveness from the Lord and myself. The Holy Spirit provided me with four insights to further my journey in recognizing the goodness of the Lord in the living world. Whenever I feel overwhelmed by thoughts suggesting that God doesn't love me because of my sins, I inquire, "Have you repented?"

If I have repented, then I would receive God's forgiveness. If I haven't repented, I must seek forgiveness.

Once I received forgiveness, the work didn't stop there. The Holy Spirit revealed three things I needed to do to harvest the Lord's goodness. I needed to wear the right gear and gloves to protect my hands when pulling lemons for the tree.

I required safety glasses and a hard hat to protect my eyes and head from falling lemons and other debris. The same is true for looking for God's goodness. I need to see my life through God's lens. I must protect my mind with the time in God's Word to show how He sees me.

The Holy Spirit last revealed to me that I need determination and focus. Picking fruit from the higher parts of the tree required me to focus on one lemon at a time. I couldn't let myself be distracted by what my friend was doing. Walking with Christ, I must fix my eyes on Jesus daily. When I concentrate on Him, I don't get drawn away by sin.

Prayer:

Lord Jesus, I cherish you and desire to be devoted to you in this life. Grant me the strength to resist sin and recognize Your goodness in all aspects of my life. Help me to embrace the whole armor of God. May I concentrate on Your boundless joy, peace, love, and kindness each day. Amen.

Your Turn:

- Have you ever deliberately sinned and wondered what you've done?
- Did you repent and ask for forgiveness?
- What did God reveal to you?
- Have you put on God's lens to see the good things in your life?

- Are your eyes **FOCUSED**—**F**ixed **O**n **C**hrist's **U**nlimited **S**upply **E**very **D**ay?

<u>Evelyn Collins</u>
Finding Courage in Chaos: Trusting God as Our Refuge in Life's Storms

*God is our refuge and strength, an ever-present help
in trouble. Therefore we will not fear, though the earth
give away and the mountains fall into the heart of the
sea, though its waters roar and foam and the
mountains quake with their surging.
Psalm 45:1-3 (NIV)*

Have you ever had a dream so realistic that you had difficulty separating reality from falsehood? I've had dreams so haunting that I was relieved to awake. Yet, certain life situations happen and feel like nightmares.

Not long ago, I dreamed of cruising a country road. Suddenly, the shiny sports car stalled. I grabbed the wheel and guided it as it slid to a stop on the grass. I abandoned the vehicle and walked along the lonely road, searching for help. Shivering in the brisk breeze, I pulled the collar of my coat tight and thrust my hands into my pockets. That's when I discovered my keys weren't there. I retraced my steps and found my car had vanished.

My dreadful dream filled me with fear. The succession of loss left my soul feeling heavy and weighed down. I've endured moments of loss, but I've never faced total despair. My dream revealed how life can change without warning.

Our dreams often mirror our deepest fears, manifesting as haunting scenarios where we find ourselves alone and stranded, grappling with helplessness and despair. These nocturnal experiences can feel all too real, stirring a sense of anxiety that lingers even after we wake. However, unlike our dreams, reality can present us with situations that are even more terrifying, situations that feel like true nightmares as we confront overwhelming challenges and loss. It's easy to feel adrift in these real-life storms, but amidst the chaos, we can find solace and strength in our faith. Only God can provide the unwavering hope we need to endure and survive life's devastating storms, reminding us that no matter how dark the path may seem, His light will guide us forward.

When Hurricane Helene struck the coast of America, powerful gusts swept rising rainwater over the land. Rivers ravaged the mountainous terrain and became mudslides. Swollen streams cut new trails across the dry land, demolishing anything in their path. Wild waves surged over the land, crushing people. The destruction was indescribable, appearing like a nightmare many wished wasn't real.

The storm left a trail of destruction when it swallowed land, collapsed structures, and snatched children from the arms of parents. Mountains which had stood for ages were powerless against the swift waters. The vicious flood devastated and displaced thousands of people when it left, leaving behind a scarred land. The storm left communities in ruins. Rivers changed the landscape of several states and the lives of surviving residents.

During tragedies like this, we may wonder where God is and how we'll recover. However, the Bible assures us that amidst life's storms,

God will always be with us, supporting us because He has a purpose for our lives.

"God is our refuge and strength, an ever-present help in trouble. Therefore we will not fear, though the earth give away and the mountains fall into the heart of the sea, though its waters roar and foam and the mountains quake with their surging" (Psalm 45:1-3, NIV).

He listens to our pleas and assists. As Christians, we serve as God's hands in the world. We must anchor ourselves in Jesus, our steadfast rock, who strengthens us during turbulent times. God is our stable foundation, enabling us to endure life's storms.

Prayer:

Dear Father, I don't know how to endure tragedy without You. God, You are my strength in both good and bad times. You give me the courage to move forward, even when I feel paralyzed with fear and doubt. Your promises will never fail, and I pray that my trust in You grows stronger. Lord, bolster my faith in the face of trials. Regardless of hardships and life's storms, please help me maintain my belief. You are the great I Am who never changes. So, I lean not on my understanding or emotions, but on Your Word. Amen.

Your Turn:

- Reflecting on past storms in your life that challenged you, what instilled bold courage during those difficult times?
- When confronted with various misfortunes, what provides you with the strength to endure?

Crystal Johnson
Restored by Grace:
My Journey Through Loss and Faith

*I will restore to you the years that the swarming locust
has eaten... You shall eat in plenty and be satisfied,
and praise the name of the Lord your God.
Joel 2:25-26 (ESV)*

Life has a way of shaking us to our core. One moment, everything is stable—our finances, home, and dreams. Then, in what seems like the blink of an eye, everything changes. I've walked that road of loss, watching what I had worked for crumble, leaving me with uncertainty and questions. In those moments of struggle, restoration felt far away. The weight of loss was heavy, and I wondered if my faith was strong enough to withstand it.

When I lost my husband, I lost more than just a partner. I lost my companion, my comforter, my provider, and my source of strength. Along with the material losses, the most profound loss was my will to live. I found myself merely existing, going through the motions of daily life without truly living. I neglected my health, skipping medications and ignoring my regular six-month doctor appointments as if none of it mattered anymore.

Experiencing Divine Restoration Beyond Loss

Like Job, who lost everything—his wealth, his health, and even his children—I found myself questioning, "Why would God allow this?" But Job's story didn't end in despair, nor did mine. Job 42:10 (ESV) says, "And the Lord restored the fortunes of Job when he had prayed for his friends. And the Lord gave Job twice as much as he had before." That verse reminded me that restoration isn't just about getting back what was lost; it's about experiencing God's grace in ways I never imagined.

In my lowest moments, I realized that my faith had been tied to what I could see like financial security, stability, good health, and comfort. But when all of that was stripped away, I found something deeper—a faith that wasn't dependent on circumstances but on God's unchanging grace.

Finding Restoration and Peace Through Faith

God didn't restore me overnight. It took time, prayer, and learning to trust Him in the wilderness. But little by little, He provided. Not just materially but spiritually. He renewed my heart, filled me with peace, and reminded me that His plans are greater than my losses. Isaiah 61:3 (ESV) speaks of God giving "a crown of beauty instead of ashes, the oil of joy instead of mourning, and a garment of praise instead of a spirit of despair." That became my reality.

If you're walking through a season of loss, I want to encourage you: God is a restorer. What you have lost does not define your future. His grace is sufficient, and His promises are true. Keep trusting. Keep believing because restoration is coming.

Prayer:

Heavenly Father, thank You for being a God of restoration who sees our pain and meets us in our brokenness. When we walk through seasons of loss, remind us that You are still in control, working all things for our good. Even when we don't understand, help us trust Your perfect plan. Lord, for those who are weary, strengthen their faith. For those who feel abandoned, remind them of Your unfailing love. For those who have lost much, restore them with material blessings, deeper peace, renewed hope, and a closer walk with You. In Jesus' name, we pray. Amen!

Your Turn:

- Have you ever experienced a season of loss that tested your faith?
- How did you respond?
- If you could encourage someone else going through loss, what would you say to them?

<u>Shai Johnson</u>
Finding Healing in God's Promise

For I will restore health unto thee, and I will heal thee
of thy wounds, saith the Lord.
Jeremiah 30:17 (KJV)

Life can be unpredictable. Some seasons feel light and joyful, while others feel like an endless cycle of hardship. When you live with chronic illness or ongoing struggles, it can be easy to feel like you're stuck in the latter. I've been in and out of hospitals since I was 13. Living with chronic illness is exhausting, not just physically but emotionally and spiritually. Some days, I feel okay, but others, I wake up wondering if I have the strength to get through it. I've prayed for healing more times than I can count. I've begged God to take away the pain, to make me whole, to let me live like everyone else. And yet, the struggles continue. It's easy to feel forgotten, to wonder if God is listening.

But then I come across a verse like Jeremiah 30:17, and I'm reminded of something important: God is a healer, not just physically but in ways much deeper than I sometimes realize. His healing isn't always instant or obvious, but it is certain. Healing isn't always about a cure. Sometimes, it's found in the strength to keep going. Sometimes, peace comes in the middle of the struggle. And sometimes, it's unexpected joy in hardship when I realize that despite it all, I'm still standing.

This verse was originally spoken to Israel, a broken and scattered people needing restoration. Yet, God's promise of healing extends beyond them. He is the same God today, still restoring, strengthening, and healing his children. Our physical, emotional, or spiritual wounds are not beyond his reach.

There have been moments when I've questioned if things will ever get better. I've cried out in frustration, like my prayers bounced off the walls. But looking back, I can also see how God has been faithful. There were moments when I felt completely alone, but a friend reached out at the right time. The days when I felt weak but somehow found the strength to push through. The nights I spent in pain, but still felt an unexplainable peace. Healing doesn't always mean an instant miracle—sometimes, God's slow and steady work renews our strength.

Remembering that healing isn't just for our physical bodies is also important. Our hearts and minds need healing, too. Maybe you've been carrying emotional wounds, past hurts, or overwhelming struggles. God's promise in Jeremiah 30:17 is for you, too. He sees your brokenness and promises restoration, even when it doesn't happen as you expect.

Maybe you're struggling with sickness, or perhaps it's another kind of wound that needs healing. Whatever it is, God sees you. He knows your pain, and he cares. Healing may not always look like we imagined, but restoration is always at work in him.

Prayer:

Heavenly Father, I come before you, bringing my wounds, struggles, and questions. Thank you for being my healer, even when I don't understand your ways. Please help me trust your restoration, find peace in your presence, and recognize your hand at work. Strengthen my faith and remind me that you are always with me. Thank you for the moments of healing, whether big or small, seen or unseen. I place my trust in you and your perfect plan. In Jesus' name. Amen.

Your Turn:

In what ways have you seen God's healing in your life, even if it wasn't the way you expected?

Andy Hollifield
Embrace the Abundance: Celebrating God's Daily Blessings and Provisions

And the children of Israel saw it, they said one to another, It is manna: for they wist not what it was. And Moses said unto them, This is the bread which the Lord hath given you to eat… And the house of Israel called the name thereof Manna: and it was like coriander seed, white; and the taste of it was like wafers made with honey.
Exodus 16:15, 31 (KJV)

I imagine that in heaven, God might say, "It's morning on earth; I should open the windows because Andy will be calling for me any minute." How wonderful would it be if we were so close to God that He expected to hear from us each morning, ready to bless us?

During the time described in Exodus, the Israelites relied on manna provided by God. Each morning, they went outside to collect this extraordinary heavenly food for their families.

Embracing Daily Blessings Through God's Faithfulness

Think about it—you could step outside each day to receive God's blessings and provisions. As Jeremiah writes in Lamentations 3:22-23 (KJV), "It is by the Lord's mercies that we are not consumed, because his compassions do not fail. They are new every morning; great is your faithfulness." Every day, the Israelites found God's blessings waiting for them. They never doubted His provision because He is faithful.

This blessing was available every morning, except on the Sabbath. On that day, they were instructed to gather twice as much the day before, prepare it, and then refrain from gathering or cooking on the Sabbath. If they tried to keep it overnight on any other day, it would spoil by morning. Isn't it comforting to know that God provides us fresh bread from heaven each day? We don't have to live on leftovers. As Psalm 68:19 (KJV) states, "Blessed be the Lord, who daily loadeth us with benefits, even the God of salvation. Selah."

Embracing New Blessings: Moving Beyond The Past

However, this raises an important question: Why do we sometimes live in the past? When we reflect on God's blessings, we often speak of what He has done in the past. I admit I am guilty of this; while those memories are cherished, they remain just that—memories. According to God's word, we need not dwell on the past. Instead, we can receive His blessings anew every morning by simply asking for them. We don't have to gather them like the Israelites did; we can pray and open our hearts to receive them.

Malachi 3:10 (KJV) speaks about tithing, stating that the Lord will "open you the windows of heaven and pour you out a blessing that there shall not be room enough to receive it." Notice that He will open "you" the windows of heaven. This means you can receive God's blessings regardless of whether others choose to.

Ephesians 3:20 (KJV) asserts, "Now unto him that is able to do exceeding abundantly above all that we ask or think, according to the power that worketh in us." I have a vivid imagination, and God can do far beyond what I can envision or request. James 4:2 (KJV) reminds us, "Ye have not because ye ask not." God desires to open the windows of heaven and pour—not sprinkle but pour—blessings on His children. Imagine how our lives could change if we woke up every morning searching for God's blessings!

The Unique Redemption of Humanity Through Christ

Jesus came to redeem fallen humanity, not animals or anything else. As Paul reiterates in 1 Corinthians 6:20 and 7:23 (KJV), we "are bought with a price," and in Ephesians 1:14 (KJV), we are referred to as a "purchased possession." This emphasizes our personal relationship with the Lord. James emphasized that "YE have not because YE ask not," targeting everyone directly, not a group.

Like the Israelites, God wants to provide us with fresh bread from heaven every day if we seek it. The window is open, and He is waiting to hear from you. He offers you "Just enough for today," but more will be there tomorrow.

Prayer:

Dear Lord, please help me have a grateful heart for all you provide me each day. Show me how to take advantage of the blessings available to me so that I can be a blessing to others. Amen.

Your Turn:

- In what ways can we cultivate a grateful heart to recognize and appreciate our blessings?

- How can we share the blessings we receive with others in our community?

Monica R. Hopper
Why Do We Believe Lies?

He has shown you, O mortal, what is good. And what
does the Lord require of you? To act justly and to love
mercy and to walk humbly with your God.
Micah 6:8 (NIV)

Politics—the word alone feels charged with emotion these days, emotions that exhaust some, embolden others, and invite a lot of frustration. I've spent my fair share of time in each of these emotions.

In 1 Samuel 8, God warned the Israelites through the prophet Samuel that having a king would lead to oppression and exploitation. The Israelites who heard Samuel's words refused to listen, just as my 7-year-old does when I instruct him to clean his lunchbox.

"But I didn't hear you!" He protests when I tell him to surrender a quarter from his money jar because of his disobedience.

Listening requires attentiveness and a desire to engage with what one hears. And listening wasn't something Israel did very well or very often. When the Israelites refused to listen to God's warning through Samuel, God told Samuel to give them the king they were begging for. He told Samuel that their demand for a king was evidence of their rejection of Him as their true King. They were no longer interested in serving God. They wanted life on their terms, with the terms of a human king. They thought serving man would be easier for them, more to their liking. They believed in a lie.

Humankind hasn't changed much, if at all. We continue to think that serving men will leave us better off. Why do we believe these lies? Maybe because we can manipulate and sway human authority. We may have specific power or control over their length and breadth of authority. Yet, we often believe humans are better at loving each other and understanding what is best for us—rather than God.

I've been reading through the minor prophets and, most recently, working through Amos. After the Lord declares judgment on some of Israel's neighbors for various things, He speaks directly to Israel and Judah (the name of the southern tribe of Israel) and proclaims judgment on them.

To Judah, He said, "...I will not revoke its punishment, because they rejected the Law of the Lord and have not kept His statutes; their lies also led them astray, those which their fathers followed. So I will send fire upon Judah, and it will consume the citadels of Jerusalem" (Amos 2:4-5, NASB2020).

To Israel, He said, "...I will not revoke its punishment, because they sell the righteous for money, and the needy for a pair of sandals. Those who trample the head of the helpless to the dust of the earth and divert the way of the humble..." (Amos 2:6-7, NASB2020).

A century later, Jeremiah, the prophet, speaks for the Lord to the Israelites. "Your affliction is incurable, your wound is severe. There is no one to plead your cause...for I have wounded you with the wound of an enemy...because your sins have increased, I have done these things to you" (Jeremiah 30:12-15, CSB).

I can't help but think as I look around—how much of this division we face daily is evidence that we would rather have a "human king" than yield our ambitions to the Creator? We in America aren't Israel, but we were made in His image all the same, and Israel as a chosen people is just a picture of what it looks like to be loved and chosen. You can be loved and chosen and blessed and have seas split before your very eyes, but what makes us belong to Him is whether we can humble ourselves, pray and seek His face, and turn from our wicked ways so that He can forgive our sin and heal our land (2 Chronicles, 7:13-14).

When I repeatedly feel discontent and powerless, I'm encouraged to listen to the Chronicler and recall the prophet Micah's instruction. "He has shown you, O mortal, what is good. And what does the Lord require of you? To act justly and to love mercy and to walk humbly with your God" (Micah 6:8, NIV). If we adhered to these principles, I believe we would choose truth rather than lies.

Prayer:

Father, I often get ideas for fixing humanity's problems that only address secondary issues. Forgive me for my tendencies to desire "a human king" more than I desire to start with the work of humbling myself, seeking You, and turning away from my sin. Thank You for your faithfulness and lead me with Your kindness. May I learn from Your Spirit how to do justice daily in a way that honors Your creation and brings glory to Your name. Amen.

Your Turn:

Psalm 20:7-8 (NIV) says, "Some trust in chariots and some in horses, but we trust in the name of the Lord our God. They are brought to their knees and fall, but we will rise up and stand firm."

- Do you find yourself with a lot of political opinions?
- As you navigate your thoughts and feelings about each conflict, is your desire for the Lord increasing, or are you looking to hold up political figures as "right"?
- How does the energy and time you spend researching, contemplating, and advocating compare to the time you spend daily walking humbly with your God, doing justice, and showing loving-kindness?
- Do you believe God can heal our land, and are you willing to seek that healing His way?

Colleen Howard
The Value of Slowing Down in a Fast-Paced World

This is the word that came to Jeremiah from the Lord:
"Go down to the potter's house, and there I will give
you my message." So, I went to the potter's house,
and I saw him working at the wheel. But the pot he
was shaping from the clay was marred in his hands;
so the potter formed it into another pot, shaping it as
seemed best to him.
Jeremiah 18:1-5 (NIV)

Several years ago, my husband and I brought home the cutest little puppy on the planet. On the third day of Miss Frankie's arrival, I tripped over the puppy gate in our kitchen and broke my femur. This was followed by an ambulance ride to the hospital, surgery, and a week of intensive physical therapy in a residential Rehab Center.

Unexpected Struggles: A Night of Relentless Pain in Rehab

Sleeping in a medical facility is often challenging, but I didn't expect this. Several days into my rehab stay, in the wee hours of the morning, a lightning bolt of pain shot from my hip to my knee to my ankle. In a continual loop, it swept over me again and again. Just as tears started running down my cheeks, I grabbed the call button to reach the nurse. Meds were administered, but the pain persisted. It was a moment of complete helplessness.

Alone in the darkness of my room, I raised my hands to the heavens, asking God for help as I waited for the meds to take effect.

Amazing Grace repeatedly played in my head as I waited for relief. The more I prayed, the more I felt God was trying to tell me something. Even through the haze of pain, I sensed it was important. Something about who I am, who He is, and what He wants me to do.

Patience: Overcoming Overachievement in Rehab

I recently realized I'm an overthinker, but I never truly faced the fact that I'm also an overachiever and highly competitive. Nothing is wrong with these qualities, but in this specific situation, God spoke clearly … *In the process of rehab, these attributes will NOT serve you well.* Amid the waiting, my precious Savior spoke directly to my heart. *Slow down. This is not a competition.* These words rolled over and over until I finally drifted off to sleep.

The next day dawned, and I reflected on this phrase—sometimes, good attributes do not apply to every situation. God whispered those nine words in my ear. Like the potter in the book of Jeremiah, God restored and reshaped my broken spirit as it seemed best to Him.

Heeding the Call to Slow Down: A Rehab Revelation

The rehab day had begun. My door flew open, and the physical therapist walked in and greeted me with a smile. We exchanged pleasantries, and I told her about my painful overnight experience. She listened intently to every detail, including every word of what God had told me. When I had finished, she said, "Didn't you hear me yesterday when I told you to slow down?"

Vaguely recalling her words, I replied, "Now that you mention it, I do remember."

Unexpected Lessons from an Unlikely Place

What an amazing Savior we serve. This lesson was a gift from God, delivered to me in this unlikely place—good attributes are not beneficial to every situation. I have learned several significant life lessons from the misstep that sent me hurling over the puppy gate.

I am in awe of how God uses everything in our lives to shape us into something better. Like the clay in the potter's hand, so are we in God's hands.

Prayer:

Dear Jesus, you are the shaper of our lives. You alone restore our hearts and renew our minds. We trust you to plan our steps and shape our lives. May the Holy Spirit guide us on the path you have prepared. Thanks be to God. Amen.

Your Turn:

Seek Him daily, and you will find Him. The potter works wonders beyond imagination. Ask the Holy Spirit to give you ears to hear, and when He whispers, take note.

- What aspects of your life might hinder how God shapes and directs you?
- Are there areas in your life where God has told you to slow down? Why? If so, how will you do this?

Andy Hollifield
When Your Hope Is Gone

*Hope deferred maketh the heart sick: but when the
desire cometh, it is a tree of life.*
Proverbs 13:12 (KJV)

In Luke 24, we find one of the saddest pictures in the bible.
Cleophas and an acquaintance were heavy-hearted as they returned
home from Jerusalem to Emmaus, about seven and a half miles away.
They began talking about the events of that week in Jerusalem. They
were soon joined by a stranger who, unbeknownst to them, was Jesus.
As he asked them what they were discussing, they gave him a rundown
of the week.

In verse 21, they tell the stranger they had trusted that Jesus would
be Israel's redeemer. Then, they explain that it had been three days
since the crucifixion. Jesus told his followers before his death that he
would raise the Tabernacle in three days. Now, their hope was lost.
Not only was their redeemer gone, but so was all Israel's hope.

Witnesses at the Tomb and Jesus' Fulfillment of Prophecy

They continued with the account of the women at the tomb seeing
the angels and being told Jesus was alive. They even told him about
Peter and John racing to the tomb only to find it empty and Jesus
nowhere to be found. In verse 25, Jesus admonishes people for not
believing what the prophets had written and said about him. He then

began expounding all the prophecies from Moses throughout all the scriptures written about him.

As they approached their home, Jesus acted like he was going on a little further. They begged him to stay with them since it was getting late. While in their home, they sat down to supper. As he took the bread, blessed it, broke it, and gave it to them, their eyes were opened, and they figured out who he was, and then he vanished.

Rekindled Hearts: The Journey Back to Jerusalem

This couple began remembering how their hearts burned as Jesus went through the scriptures. They immediately returned to Jerusalem, even though it was probably already evening and close to dark. They found the disciples and other followers of Jesus gathered, discussing Christ's appearance with Peter.

While they told their experience to those gathered, Jesus appeared in the midst. Even though they knew he'd risen, they were still scared and thought they saw a spirit. Jesus first showed them his wounds, but they still wondered about it. He still had to convince them it was him in the flesh and not a spirit by eating fish and honeycomb. As Jesus ate, he reminded them of the scriptures written about him by the prophets. He opened their understanding so they could comprehend the meaning of the scriptures. Then he began to explain they were witnesses of all that both he and the prophets had spoken. After Jesus blessed them, they worshipped him with great joy.

From Despair to Jubilation: Finding Hope in Jesus

I went over this whole story to illustrate that with Jesus, there's always hope. Things aren't always what they seem. These folks had spent over a week seeing their greatest fears be realized when Jesus was arrested, tried, and crucified. Many had devoted their lives to Jesus over his three-plus years of ministry. They were now disillusioned at best and distraught or worse. Their hope had died on that cross. For the last ten days, their situation had gone from bad to worse with the arrest and trials to completely hopeless with his crucifixion. Now, they couldn't believe their eyes! What, only moments before, had been heartbreaking and hopeless had now become total jubilation.

You may've reached a place where your hope is gone. Common sense tells you your situation is beyond hope. Effort and rational thought have proven there's no help for it. Your heart and mind want to hope and believe, but your circumstances say it's useless. You've reached the same place these folks had. I hope this has helped you realize that with Jesus, there's never a time when your hope is gone. "For with God, nothing shall be impossible" (Luke 1:37, KJV).

Prayer:

Dear Father, thank you for dying on the cross for me and creating the ability to live a restored life through you. Please renew my mind when I struggle with despair, discouragement, and doubt. Amen.

Your Turn:

- Have you ever struggled with hopelessness and doubt?
- How did you recover if you've ever reached a place in your life when your hope was gone?

Terrance Niedziela Jr.
Where's Your Citizenship?

*Then the commander came and said to him, "Tell me,
are you a Roman?" He said, "Yes." The commander
answered, "With a large sum, I obtained this
citizenship." And Paul said, "But I was born a citizen.*
Acts 22:27-28 (NKJV)

*Now, therefore, you are no longer strangers and
foreigners, but fellow citizens with the saints and
members of the household of God.*
Ephesians 2:19 (NKJV)

Citizenship comes with rewards and responsibilities. Citizens receive the protection of the country's government and military, vote, serve in the military, receive social security and other financial benefits, and hold public offices. In many countries, citizens receive free healthcare.

Paul's readers understood citizenship. The Roman Empire protected its citizens, and anyone who messed with them faced serious consequences. Roman citizens had the right to appeal to Caesar and have him try their case. This is why the centurion and those who would beat Paul in Acts 22:27-28 were afraid when they found out he was a Roman.

Embracing Your Identity as a Member of God's Household

In Ephesians 2:19 (NKJV), Paul wrote, "Now, therefore, you are no longer strangers and foreigners, but fellow citizens with the saints and members of the household of God."

The Lord Jesus makes His disciples saints and members of God's family. God is the High King of Heaven. His children are citizens of the Kingdom of Heaven. We are also made the righteousness of God in Christ Jesus, protected by angels who obey the Word of God (Psalm 103:20, NKJV), heirs of a rich inheritance made kings and priests ambassadors of Christ, and so on.

Prioritizing God's Kingdom Over Worldly Affairs

Since we are citizens of God's kingdom and heaven, God's agenda is more important to us than any other. One of the things the enemy has deceived us into focusing on is the affairs of this world. We get so caught up in our life drama, politics, and all the other stuff going on in the world, and we forget that this world isn't even home.

The kingdom of darkness controls the world we live in. The things that it considers important are considered an abomination to God (Luke 16:15, NKJV). We often focus on things that have no true importance in the light of eternity. At the same time, the kingdom of darkness claims one soul after another. Therefore, in Revelation, Jesus could say to the church that He did not find works complete in His sight.

The Primacy of Heavenly Citizenship Responsibilities

The Lord has shown me many places where I am guilty of this. Our Lord will bring us home soon, and we will all have to give an account of whether we carried out the responsibilities of our faithful citizenship. All this is not to say that we must neglect our citizenship duties here on earth. There are things we need to make sure we're doing. But the responsibilities of our Heavenly citizenship are more important.

Prayer:

Heavenly Father, thank You for adopting us and making us citizens of Your heavenly kingdom. Please forgive me for not treating my citizenship with more respect. Please give me mercy and grace to live as a citizen of heaven. May my refocused life bring glory to You and bring the lost into Your kingdom. In Jesus' name. Amen.

Your Turn:

- How will knowing about being a citizen of God's kingdom with benefits and responsibilities change how you see your current circumstances?
- How has focusing on earthly citizenship stopped you from fulfilling heavenly responsibilities?
- With the Holy Spirit's guidance and empowerment, how will you align one area of your life with the Word of God to behave as a citizen of heaven?

Lilka Finely Raphael
Restoration

He restores my soul; He leads me in the paths of
righteousness. For His name's sake.
Psalms 23:3 (NKJV)

Though I was very familiar with Psalm 23, I recognized something for the first time. The third verse describing God's restoration lies between a reference to "still waters" and a "walk through the valley of the shadow of death." These are vastly different circumstances.

Perhaps our ability to navigate life's treacherous journeys is found in choosing to be still despite our hectic lives. Even Jesus left the crowds and His disciples to enter quiet time with the Father.

Life is challenging. Current events drain our energy. Yet, our God offers rest and restoration that equips us for the worrisome seasons to come. Our emotional and mental fatigue are alleviated when we accept the opportunity for renewal. The psalmist's verse concerning restoration immediately follows the reference to still waters. God's word is not random. Our merciful Father sustains us with His living water.

Unfortunately, we don't always follow. We easily dismiss the Spirit's promptings in our misguided quests to find restoration through people and things. We cannot hear God when our minds are muddled with pings, dings, and outside chatter. But in quiet times free of distractions, we can recognize the Lord's paths of righteousness—His plans and our purpose.

God's direction toward tranquil spaces offers peace that is otherwise unobtainable. He offers an oasis in our deserts that we cannot create alone. God strengthens us not merely spiritually, but emotionally and physically as well. Our bodies often reflect what is churning beneath the surface.

Many of us struggle through our challenging times, defeated and hopeless. We may win an occasional battle, but we can never win the war without the Lord. We don't deserve God's mercy, but our Father restores and guides His children for His name's sake.

Everything we need is found in Him. When we choose to be still and subsequently refreshed, we can recognize the paths of righteousness our Father would have us follow.

Never fear, God offers the restoration that allows us to walk confidently through dark places.

Prayer:

Heavenly Father, I come before You with a grateful heart, seeking restoration during my struggles. I ask for our gentle hand to heal my soul, to mend the broken places within me, and to grant me peace in the chaos of life. Help me to find stillness in Your presence, where I can hear Your voice guiding me along the paths of righteousness. I trust that You are with me, even in my darkest moments, providing strength and hope when I feel weary. Lord, renew my spirit and refresh my mind as I surrender my burdens to You. Thank You for Your unwavering love and mercy; may I always walk confidently in the light of Your assurance. Amen.

Your Turn:

- In what ways do we often seek restoration from external sources rather than turning to God for the peace and renewal we truly need?

- How can we intentionally create moments of stillness in our daily lives to better perceive God's guidance and presence amidst our challenges?

Colleen Howard
Eyes on the Road

*I focus on this one thing: Forgetting the past and
looking forward to what lies ahead, I press on to
reach the end of the race and receive the heavenly
prize for which God, through Christ Jesus, is calling
us.*
Philippians 3:13-14 (NLT)

What will today look like? Will it disappoint? Will our dreams come true? Of course, none of us knows the answer, but I know someone who does. God has gifted us with another new day, and like a roadmap, it's filled with possibilities. Are you ready to let the adventure begin, or does it seem intimidating?

Since I've already started down the road trip trail, let's look at the rearview mirror vs the windshield. One is for looking at what's behind, and the other is to see what lies before. If you want to arrive safely at your destination, you glance out the rearview mirror, but your number one focus is on the road ahead. It's a little like life. If we spend too much time looking back, we might miss our exit.

In Garth Stein's book, The Art of Racing in the Rain, the main character is a racecar driver who states, "In racing, they say that your car goes where your eyes go. The driver who cannot tear his eyes away from the wall as he spins out of control will meet that wall; the driver who looks down the track as he feels his tires break free will regain control of his car."

When I learned to drive, I was told to keep my eyes on the road. If something falls from the passenger seat onto the car's floor and you look down to retrieve it, your vehicle will most likely veer off track. This happens because your car goes where your eyes are focused. It's like what racecar drivers call *racing in the rain*.

But aren't we all racing in the rain? Don't we often spend too much time dwelling on the past and not enough looking forward to the future? In driving, the rearview mirror serves a specific purpose, and looking back briefly is not bad. However, too much time focused on the rearview will alter your course. It's the view out of the windshield that drives us forward.

God is continually beckoning us to follow, and He is worthy of our loyalty. He holds our future, and His view is eternal. Occasionally, bumps in the road will slow us down, but whatever the speed, life keeps moving forward. We cannot stop or pause time, but can place our trust in Jesus Christ. God has strategically placed you right where you are supposed to be. Let's keep our eyes on Jesus. He is our rock and refuge and will reposition us if we swerve off the road.

The next time you fling that car door open and sit behind the wheel, pray boldly to the God who holds the map. Every day belongs to Him. As you wait expectantly for the treasures He will reveal down the road, keep moving forward, eyes on the road, and know whatever comes your way is most assuredly in His hands.

Prayer:

Dear Jesus, remind us daily to look forward to what lies ahead and focus on the path you have laid before us. Help us not to spend too much time in the past, but to persevere until we reach the end of the race. May your Spirit guide us toward a deeper relationship with you. Thanks be to God. Amen

Your Turn

- When you reflect on the past, do you see where you needed more focus? How did God reposition you back on the road?
- What did you learn from this experience, and how will that affect your future decisions?

Kathy Keenum
A Sculptor's Hands

*Therefore, if anyone is in Christ, he is a new
creation; old things have passed away; behold, all
things have become new.
2 Corinthians 5:17 (NKJV)*

Sand flows across the beach, painting ever-changing images from the water's edge to the dunes. The grains of sand are loose, not held together, which allows them to be blown around, at the mercy of the wind. The grains can create beautiful images or ripples across the beach to the dunes. The beach can be peaceful, chaotic, attractive, and ugly, but always different.

The Art of Transformation: From Loose Sand to Masterful Sculpture

When a sculptor works with grains of sand, a transformation occurs. The once loose sand at the mercy of the wind becomes part of something incredible. The skilled hands of the sculptor mold those grains, creating a wonderful image. What's produced is an image greater than any individual grain, crafted by the master. No longer is the sand being blown about. It's now part of something great.

Before a person becomes a Christ follower, their life is like that grain of sand. They lack the proper focus. They can be blown or influenced by all the things of the world. Their mission isn't aligned with God's—only after what pleases them. The wind no longer blows us once Christ sculpts us into His image. We have become part of the wonderful image the master has crafted. We now have a Christ-like focus, purpose, and mission.

Transformation Through Christ: Becoming a New Creation

Paul wrote in Corinthians that we are a new creation once we follow Christ. Our old life passes away. Christ transforms us. We do not crave the things of the world, but begin to crave becoming more Christ-like. This transformation is a continual process, but the changes in our lives become evident to those around us.

Paul's insights on these changes show they are not superficial but fundamental to each person.

Understanding Our Identity in Christ

1. In Christ: This refers to Christ Followers—those with a personal relationship with the Lord. Paul uses this verse to encourage believers. There is always a temptation to sin or backslide into our old nature. So, we must work on strengthening our relationship with the Lord.

2. New Creation: When we begin a relationship with Christ, we become a new person. It is a radical change. The Lord forgives our sins. We are different. This will become evident in how we act, the words we use, the things we do, even the places we go. Others will notice this change.

3. Old has gone: We are transformed from our old life to a new life centered around Christ. We are no longer the same person we were. Our old life is gone. We begin living differently,

acting differently, and wanting different things. The changes are obvious to those around us.

Prayer:

Lord, please guide me as I walk daily in Christ. Draw close to me so I can avoid temptation. May it be evident to those around me that I have transformed my life. Direct my decisions so they are centered on Godly things. Please allow my life to glorify you in all I say and do. Amen.

Your Turn:

- Do you have a personal relationship with Christ?
- Has your life been changed?
- Does your life glorify the Lord?

Vonyee K. Carrington
Renovated from the Inside Out:
Finding God in the Mess and the Makeover

*But now thus says the Lord, he who created you, O
Jacob, he who formed you, O Israel: Fear not, for I
have redeemed you; I have called you by name, you
are mine . . . Remember not the former things nor
consider the things old. Behold, I am doing something
new; now it springs forth, do you not perceive it? I
will make a way in the wilderness and rivers in the
desert.*
Isaiah 43:1, 18-19 (ESV)

I moved into my home several years ago. The kitchen was the only area I didn't change before moving in. I thought, "I'll do it within the first year."

The first year comprised finding a new church and a new job. The second year involved finding a new job and getting involved at my church. In the third and fourth years, I returned to the challenge of finding the next job. In year five, water problems (a hole in a well pipe, an issue with my home water filtration system, and a flooded yard) consumed my existence. 2025 began, and I thought, "I can work on the kitchen," yet there is an impending recession.

I decided to forge ahead with my kitchen redo. If you've ever undertaken any renovation, you know it is a process. My process has been in five steps:

1. The first step is planning and decision-making. You meet with the designer. You figure out what you want and what you don't

want. It is also the step where you decide how much the project will cost. As I've gone through the planning process, I have thought about how this phase has a spiritual aspect. For Christians, the planning phase is equal to the phase where you count the cost of the endeavor. Luke 14:28 (NLT) reminds us to "...don't begin until you count the cost." Who would begin construction of a building without first calculating the cost? Not only do you count the cost, but you also begin to seek God, His strength, and His Presence (1 Chronicles 16:11). Since God is our Master Designer, you also listen. You listen for directions on how to complete the task. You're listening for God's stamp of approval.

2. The second step in the renovation process is packing and removing items. My kitchen is not huge. However, I do have many items. I started asking myself, "Do I use this item? How often do I use this item? Do I need it in my life? Will it be cheaper to keep the item or buy something newer at the end of the process? Am I committed to a kitchen renovation?" I've asked similar questions when God is renovating my life. It is getting rid of items that make the renovation more real. I must be fully committed to following God's course for my life.

3. After the packing and getting rid of the old comes the demolition phase. Cabinets, countertops, and light fixtures are torn out and thrown away. The same thing happens in my spiritual walk. I allow God to come in and clear away all the old debris. 2 Corinthians 7:1 (ESV) encourages us "...cleanse ourselves from every defilement of body and spirit, bringing

holiness to completion." I implement new practices and new mindsets to move forward in God.

4. An empty space follows the demolition phase. You stand in the barren area, wondering if you did the right thing, knowing there's no turning back. For me, this is the hardest stage. I am more susceptible to the wiles of the devil. I must "set my mind on the things that are above, not on things that are on earth" (Colossians 3:2, ESV). I decide not to look at the barrenness, but to look at God's goodness in my life.

5. Installation follows demolition. Floors are installed. I now have a firm foundation. Cabinets go in place to store treasures, not just physical treasures but also spiritual ones. Lights are placed so that the whole of the room is illuminated. The last part of the renovation is viewing the completed project. Completion brings a new space and a sense of peace. In the renovation phase, you can embrace God's word that He's doing a new thing.

In the journey of faith, the renovation of our spiritual lives can be likened to a home improvement project, reflecting five key steps:

1. **Planning and Decision-Making:** Just as we meet with a designer to envision our renovation, we must seek God's guidance, counting the cost of discipleship (Luke 14:28) and listening for His direction.

2. **Packing and Removing Items:** As we declutter our physical space, we must also evaluate what is essential in our spiritual

lives. Shedding the unnecessary paves the way for a more committed walk with Christ.

3. **Demolition:** The demolition phase allows God to remove the old habits and sins that hinder us. We cleanse ourselves from every defilement to make room for holiness (2 Corinthians 7:1).

4. **Barren Space:** After demolition, we often face a void that can be daunting. In this stage, we're reminded to focus on God's goodness rather than our circumstances (Colossians 3:2).

5. **Installation and Completion:** Finally, as we build up again with strength and purpose, we welcome God's new blessings and clarity. Completion fosters peace, allowing us to nurture and use the gifts He has given us (2 Timothy 1:6).

Remembering these steps, we can confidently embrace our spiritual renovation, knowing that each phase brings us closer to the life God has designed for us. When renovated from the inside out, we'll find God in the mess *and* the makeover.

Prayer:

As I embark on this personal transformation, I invite Lord Jesus into every part of my life. I recognize that renovation requires deep changes, and I pray for the strength to embrace them. Help me see Your goodness throughout this journey, even in challenges. Guide my thoughts and actions, allowing me to trust Your process and timing. May this transformation change my circumstances, heart, and mind. Thank you, Lord, for supporting me as I seek renewal. Amen.

Your Turn:

- Have you started any new projects recently? It's essential to consider the excitement and the costs involved—time and resources.

- Have you recognized the treasures or skills God has given you to help with these endeavors? Also, reflect on whether you've let go of old mindsets that might be holding you back.

- Are you fully committed to your new perspectives? That commitment is key to transformation.

- Are you allowing God to guide you in completing your projects? Trusting in this process can lead to fulfillment beyond mere success. Embrace the journey and stay open to new possibilities.

<u>Evelyn Collins</u>
When Everything Falls Apart—What Do You Do?

Therefore, if anyone is in Christ, the new creation has come: The old has gone, the new is here!
2 Corinthians 5:17 (NIV)

Can you remember a time when you felt wounded beyond repair? The world collapsed around you and threatened to rob you of joy. Your life, once vibrant and full of promise, lay in shattered fragments at your feet. How do you navigate the arduous journey from brokenness to healing? Wholeness emerges when you redirect your gaze away from the chaos of others and the turmoil of your circumstances, focusing instead on a higher purpose, on God. Then life changes, and good things happen. In that profound shift of perspective, life transforms, and unexpectedly beautiful moments unfold again.

Understanding the Misalignment of Focus in Seeking Divine Intervention

Years ago, I cried to the Lord, begging Him to change my life. Since I sought the Lord in prayer, I felt my focus was on Him, not realizing I focused on my problem rather than Christ. I sought God's intervention, not His will. Struggling, I remained in a miserable marriage, because I thought He wanted me to stay in it. "Marriage is a lifetime commitment," I would repeat to myself. I quit my job, and we sold our home. My husband at the time and I took our girls several states away from family and friends. But life did not change for the better—our marriage failed. God didn't intervene or restore our marriage.

The heartache I felt being in a new town without family or friends, while my marriage failed, devastated me. Glowing embers of love faded into ashes. Broken vows and abandoned dreams died. Through the bitterness of unfaithfulness, I discovered God's faithfulness. He placed me in a job surrounded by supportive Christian friends and a wonderful church.

Guided by the Spirit of God, these individuals helped me recognize my true value and potential. They demonstrated God's love toward me and supported me during a challenging period. They became like family, encouraging me to embrace my new identity in Christ and walk forward in His grace (2 Corinthians 5:17).

Finding Strength and Security Through Faith in God

With my life in God's hands, my heart and mind focused on Him alone, I desired nothing else. When I lean on God, I'm stronger and more secure because God loves me. I expect great things from my life. While change is challenging, the rewards are worth it.

I learned several things from this difficult season in life.

- Praying to God doesn't mean seeking Him or His will.
- God may not change our circumstances, but He can change us.
- Seek God's direction, rather than relying on emotions, wisdom, or strength.

- Restoration begins when we yield to God's will and walk in obedience.
- God is faithful, even if hardship results from disobedience or failure to surrender.
- Lean on His strength rather than our weakness.

Finding Purpose Through Trusting God

Days of pain and heartache are much a part of this world. Our trust is in God, both now and for eternity. When we receive Christ as our savior, his spirit is with us each day of our lives. God did not design us to depend upon our ability.

When we surrender to God, He heals us and brings joy and purpose. When we feel weak, we can still face each day with God's strength. He wants us to depend on him. God often chooses the weak, so others recognize His power in accomplishing the work. So, with each success, we conclude a miracle occurred—to God be the glory!

Prayer:

Lord, thank You for Your loving care and for directing me on the right path. Forgive me for seeking to go alone rather than ask for guidance. Help me surrender my will and accept the divine path before me. I pray my pleas for help include "thy will be done" because I can't understand the way to go without revelation from above. Amen.

Your Turn:

When have you felt your world collapse around you? It's a question many of us can relate to at different points in our lives. For me, it was during a particularly tumultuous period filled with disappointments and challenges that seemed insurmountable. It felt as though everything I had built—relationships, dreams, and security—was crumbling away, leaving me in a state of despair. During that troubling time, did you call upon the Lord? What were your words to Him, and His response?

In those moments of darkness, I found myself turning to prayer. I remember being on my knees, feeling vulnerable and lost. My words to the Lord were raw and honest; I spoke of my fears, my pain, and my feelings of abandonment. "Why is this happening to me? Why do I feel so alone?" I begged for guidance, strength, and a sense of peace that felt utterly out of reach. Get honest before God. What specific guidance, strength, and peace do you need right now?

<u>Crystal Johnson</u>
From Broken to Brand New

*Therefore, if anyone is in Christ, the new creation has
come: The old has gone, the new is here!*
2 Corinthians 5:17 (NIV)

The Power of a Fresh Start

There's something incredibly empowering about beginning anew. Whether it's the start of a new year, a fresh job, or simply a new day after a difficult night, the concept of a fresh start brings a sense of hope. However, the newness described by Paul in 2 Corinthians 5:17 goes far beyond merely resetting or getting a second chance. It speaks to transformation, an internal renewal that fundamentally reshapes who we are.

This verse resonates with me because I understand what it feels like to carry the burden of an "old self." I recall times when shame followed me like a shadow, and I defined myself by errors and wrong turns. There were aspects of my life I wanted to keep hidden, parts I attempted to cover up with busyness, distractions, or even religious acts. But none of those strategies succeeded.

Understanding What It Means to Be "In Christ"

It wasn't until I truly grasped what it meant to be "in Christ" that I began to experience absolute freedom. Being in Christ is more than believing in Him. It involves letting his life become my own. It means adopting a new identity that isn't tied to my past but is grounded in his grace and redemption. Paul is communicating this: when we unite with

Jesus, our entire spiritual essence transforms. We're not just improved versions of our old selves; we become entirely new.

What's remarkable is that this "new creation" isn't just a metaphor or pleasant religious talk. It's a tangible, lived reality. I recall when I started viewing my life through this perspective. The things that once held me captive, like fear, resentment, and even harmful relationships, began to lose their power over me. I didn't transform overnight, but I had a newfound awareness and strength that hadn't existed before.

Desires Renewed by Christ

I began to desire different things. My heart became more compassionate. I wanted to love people more deeply and live with greater purpose. This wasn't about self-improvement but Christ's Spirit working within me. The old habits, thoughts, and false beliefs I held about myself started to diminish. Yes, they still occasionally whisper, but they no longer define who I am.

The beauty of this verse lies in its message: it doesn't say, "If someone is good enough," or "If someone gets their act together," then they become a new person. It states, "If anyone is in Christ." This means the promise is available to everyone, regardless of past mistakes or how far we've strayed. It's not about our actions but what Jesus has done and continues to do in us.

You Are Not Stuck—There Is Hope

Perhaps you're like I was, burdened with guilt from your past or feeling trapped by your former self. Maybe you've tried to change repeatedly, only to fall into the same habits. If this resonates with you, let me gently remind you: you don't have to remain in that place. Jesus offers not only forgiveness but transformation. He doesn't just wipe the slate clean; He gives you a new life.

Embracing this new identity requires time and effort. It involves spending time with Jesus through prayer and scripture, allowing his truth to replace the falsehoods we've believed. It also means surrounding ourselves with a community that supports growth and accountability. It involves trusting that God is still at work within us, even on challenging days, reshaping our hearts to reflect his nature.

So, live like it. Lean into it. Let grace shape you.

- Reflect on where God has brought you from.
- Thank Him for who he's making you into.
- Share this truth with someone who needs a fresh start.

Prayer:

Heavenly Father, thank you for the promise of new life through Christ. Thank you for that. I am not bound by my past or defined by my mistakes. You make all things new, and You are faithfully transforming me day by day. Help me walk in my new identity, let go of shame, and embrace Your grace. Empower me to be a living testimony of your love and renewal, and give me courage to share this hope with others. In Jesus' name. Amen.

Your Turn:

- In what areas of your life do you still feel defined by your "old self"?

- What would it look like to truly live from your identity as a new creation in Christ?
- Who needs to hear the hope that transformation is possible through Jesus?

Colleen Howard
Do You Really Know God?

*Have I not commanded you? Be strong and
courageous. Do not be frightened, and do not be
dismayed, for the Lord your God is with you wherever
you go.*
Joshua 1:9 (ESV)

The phrase "God is with us" is a familiar promise appearing numerous times in the Bible. In Matthew 28:20 (ESV), God tells us, "I am with you always, to the end of the age." He is unchanging and faithful, His love is never-ending, and His promises are true. This indicates that we're in a state of togetherness *with* the Lord. *Withness* is a gift from God to those who follow Him. He goes before us, walks *with* us, and prepares a place for us at His table.

How do we participate in the withness?

God asks us to be doers of the word by sharing the Gospel. He instructs us to write His words on our hearts, pray with Him, and be witnesses for Jesus Christ, our Lord and Savior.

In 1 Peter 3:18 (ESV), God's Word says, "But grow in the grace and *knowledge* of our Lord and Savior Jesus Christ." The good news is, our God doesn't ask anything of us without first equipping us for the job. He designed us to live in a community with brothers and sisters in Christ. He gave us hearts to encourage each other, share our victories and defeats, and comfort others in need. God has given us the Holy Spirit, who guides our steps along the path He prepared beforehand (Ephesians 2:10, ESV). He designed us to be *with* Him and to *know* Him.

What does it mean to know God?

Many say they "know" God, but in truth, they only know "about" Him. There is a difference between knowing *about* God and *knowing* God. Have you experienced His goodness (Psalm 34:8), the comfort of His words (Psalm 34:18), and the overwhelming peace you feel in His presence (Romans 15:13)?

Let's break it down — most of us know about honey, but there's a difference between *knowing* honey and knowing *about* honey. Those who know *about* it can list the facts. It's a sweet liquid produced by bees from the nectar of flowers. It's often used in cooking as a spread or sweetener. Almost anyone can recite these well-known facts about honey.

However, to *know* honey, you must experience it. Have you drizzled honey over a warm slice of freshly baked bread and licked the sticky, sweet substance from your fingers? Have you tasted the goodness of honey cake or the tangy delight of soy-honey-ginger sauce lightly covering your perfectly grilled salmon?

Many people claim to *know* God, but some only *know about* Him. When you "know" God, you share your struggles, doubts, and hopes with Him. You trust Him, and His presence, power, and promises are the foundation of your life. Knowing the heart of God changes everything because He is "with" you.

Experiencing His presence is life-changing. Perhaps you've seen God's fingerprints on your life when walking through a wilderness season. He is with us always, and His presence sustains us. Psalm 63:3 (TPT) tells us, "For your tender mercies mean more to me than life itself."

God calls you every day. He knocks at the door of your heart. But He's not just knocking at your door — He's knocking down your fears, secrets, loneliness, anger, bitterness, trauma, and sorrows. The God who holds the planets in orbit, and knows the name of every star offers you a love like no other. It's an invitation to the most incredible adventure you'll ever encounter—*withness*.

If you haven't *experienced* God, invite Him into every corner of your heart. The more you see Him, the more you seek Him. The more you seek Him, the more you know Him.

Prayer:

Dear Jesus, help us remember how you have provided for us. Let us be immersed in your love and mesmerized by your unfailing love. Never forget that God is *with* you always and will never abandon you. Thank you, Father God, for showing us how to see you, seek you, and truly know your heart. Praise be to God. Amen.

Your Turn:

Psalm 77:11-12 tells us to remember the deeds God has done and meditate on them.

- Did you sense His presence, hear His whisper?

- How did He get your attention?
- What faith-steps can you take today to deepen your knowledge of God?

Shai Johnson
Torn—To Be—Healed

Come, let us return to the Lord; for he has torn us,
that he may heal us: he has struck us down, and he
will bind us up.
Hosea 6:1 (ESV)

Living with illness or enduring difficult seasons of life can often make us question everything. Why does suffering exist? Why do we have to go through such hard times? Why would a loving God allow us to endure pain and hardship? These are the questions I wrestle with daily. Since I was young, I've had to live with my health struggles, chronic conditions that seem always to be there, lingering and never truly leaving. Though there are moments when I feel good, it's often followed by periods of pain, exhaustion, and frustration. In those moments, I've wondered, "Where is God in all of this? How can a loving God allow this much suffering?"

Reconciling the Paradox of Divine Love and Suffering

Hosea 6:1 (ESV) speaks directly to this tension: "He has torn us, that he may heal us." At first, it feels hard to reconcile the idea of a loving God allowing us to be torn down. How can God, who promises love, also strike us down? Doesn't love protect? Doesn't love heal immediately?

The truth I'm slowly coming to realize is that God's love isn't always what we expect. Sometimes, the path to healing is through struggle. Sometimes, healing takes time, and the process isn't easy. It doesn't mean God loves us any less; it means He's at work in deeper ways than we often see.

Embracing God's Mysterious Path to Healing

God's healing often comes in unexpected ways. It's not always immediate or obvious. We may not see the results we want right away, but that doesn't mean healing isn't taking place. It might be that we're healed in our hearts before we're healed in our bodies. It might mean that the healing process takes time, requiring us to trust in God's plan even when unsure of what that looks like.

There are moments when I feel completely torn apart by my illness, my pain, and my doubts. But when I step back and look at the bigger picture, I can see that God is at work in ways I didn't expect. I've learned that He doesn't waste our pain. Though I don't have all the answers or understand the reasons behind the struggles, I can trust that God is always at work, even in the hardest moments.

Embracing the Journey: Finding Healing Through Struggle

Sometimes, the struggle itself is part of God's healing process. We don't always understand how God works, but we can trust that He's using the pain to shape us into something more whole, more refined. Healing doesn't always look like we imagine. Sometimes, it's the inner strength that arises in the middle of the pain. Other times, it's the peace we feel amid uncertainty. And sometimes, the unexpected moments of joy come even when circumstances are hard.

God is not distant. He is with us, walking alongside us through every painful moment, holding us when we feel broken, and lifting us when we feel like we can't stand. He has torn us, but He will bind us up again. The process may be painful, but it leads to restoration. Healing is not always instant, but it is certain. God is in the business of restoring His children, in ways both seen and unseen.

Prayer:

Dear God, I come to you with a heart full of questions and struggles. Sometimes it's hard to understand why the healing takes so long or the journey feels so painful. Help me trust that you are with me, even in the darkest times. Remind me that your love for me is not just in the moments of comfort, but also in the moments of pain and growth. Strengthen my faith, even when I don't have all the answers, and help me trust your perfect timing and love. In Jesus' name, Amen.

Your Turn:

How can you invite God into your moments of struggle, trusting that His presence can bring healing, even if the answers aren't clear yet?

Monica Hopper
Mercy for the Bird:
A Playdate, a Prayer, and God's Promise

...He causes His sun to rise on the evil and the good,
and sends rain on the righteous and the unrighteous.
Matthew 5:45 (NIV)

Anticipation crackled in the air, reaching a fever pitch as the playdate unfolded, promising a whirlwind of unforgettable adventures. Twelve kids running around our property were suddenly less interested in the bounce house, the kickball game, and climbing trees—the barn cats had a bird.

The girls rescued a bird, probably a fledgling since it would occasionally stand up, and brought it to me. It didn't look well, but it was chirping. I debated a merciful death, but I didn't have it in me. It didn't show any external wounds, and I was unwilling to assume its condition required a dramatic end with six girls looking on. The girls made a nest and placed it in the garage, away from the cats.

Planting Seeds of Hope Amid Unexpected Interruptions

My husband and I had set aside a precious 5-hour block that afternoon for a work date, a time meant for tackling mentally challenging tasks without the distractions of our children. However, our plans were interrupted by the chirping of a hungry fledgling in the garage. Returning her to the nest high in the barn seemed futile—she'd already endured a fall and had been separated from her mother. Our options were limited with four curious barn cats roaming the property and the nearest rehabilitation center two hours away. Yet, in that moment, we offered a prayer, reflecting on the care of a heavenly Father whose eye is on the sparrow (Matt. 10:29). With renewed purpose, we rose from our work and picked up a spade, ready to plant seeds of hope and compassion in the flower bed.

Immediately, three worms were evident. The hungry bird would eat.

I contemplated this small miracle all day. I weeded and planted in those beds three weeks ago, and for the most part, found no worms. For the first slight turn of a spade to show forth three worms, nearly on the surface, was the merciful hand of a bird's heavenly Father.

Paul beautifully describes the goal of God's merciful hand in our lives when he wrote, "…do you think lightly of the riches of His kindness and restraint and patience, not knowing that the kindness of God leads you to repentance?" (Romans 2:4, NASB)

Recognizing Divine Intervention in Everyday Moments

What a question to consider. Do we take for granted those moments when He helps us find that item we were desperately searching for, when the phone call we have been dreading is surprisingly uplifting, when the merciful cancellation of a meeting or requirement temporarily calms our chaotic work-life balance? Oh! The temptation to see these items as chance happenings—*and not the calling from our Lord to repentance of our independence*—is strong!

The world is no help. It is blatant and insistent in its messaging to deny God's existence and engagement: "The stars aligned!" "The universe brought us together!" "Manifest your destiny!" "Positive vibes only!"

God's Timeless and Trustworthy Nature

But God is not threatened. His character and messaging are both timeless and trustworthy. In His great mercy, "He causes His sun to rise on the evil and the good, and sends rain on the righteous and the unrighteous" (Matt 5:45, NIV). With that same mercy, He calls us out of our doubt and into the joy of knowing Him (Romans 11:28-36).

And so, we who he calls can please Him in our response! As Hebrews 11:6 (NIV) tells us, "Without faith it is impossible to please God, because anyone who comes to Him must believe that He exists and that He rewards those who earnestly seek Him."

Proclaiming God's Sovereignty in Everyday Miracles

Each moment and area of our lives is a realm where we are invited to announce His sovereignty and declare His goodness and mercy. When God provides for the vehicle your family desperately needs, you find that item you thought you lost, or when your father says, "I love you," after years of shutting you out, you have that opportunity for a counter-cultural message. God did what I could not do. His mercies are "new every morning," and the riches of knowing Him and being loved by Him far surpass the world's empty promises (Lamentations 3:22-23, ESV).

Prayer:

Give me eyes to see, Lord, and ears to listen to You. May I marvel at your mercies, both small and significant! Please help me to confess my unbelief and invite you to renew my mind. May I embrace the joy of knowing You as the first and greatest mercy, through which I can discover hope for each new day. Amen.

Your Turn:

- What mercies of God have you experienced?
- How do you honor the Lord's mercy in your life?
- Do you declare His goodness publicly when His mercy is shown to you, or do you breathe a sigh of relief when you experience His mercy and then wrestle the doubt beast down, quickly moving along to the next thing?
- What does God want from you now?
- How can you honor Him?

Terrance Niedziela Jr.
God Removes Shame and Its Source

*Instead of your shame you shall have double honor,
And instead of confusion they shall rejoice in their
portion. Therefore in their land they shall possess
double; Everlasting joy shall be theirs.
Isaiah 61:7 (NKJV)*

Ever since Adam's sin, every human has experienced the shame and devastation of doing and speaking evil. I have lost a great deal because of my past sins. I have wondered—Can I ever live without the shame of my past? Is it possible to get back what I lost? Isaiah 61:7 is one of many scriptures that answer these questions. The prophet Isaiah wrote, "Instead of your shame you shall have double honor, And instead of confusion they shall rejoice in their portion. Therefore in their land they shall possess double; Everlasting joy shall be theirs" (NKJV).

God not only removes the feelings of shame we experience from sinning, but also the cause of the shame.

Understanding the Concept of Shame and Its Removal Through Faith

The word "shame" used in this passage is *bosheth* and means "shame or shameful thing."[2] It comes from the Hebrew word *buwsh*, which means "the feeling and condition, as well as the cause of shame, an idol".[3] God not only removes the feelings of shame we experience from sinning, but also the cause of the shame. Shame drives us away from God, not toward Him. We shrink away and think we must "clean ourselves up" before we enter His presence. I have met people who say, "Once I get my life right, I'll go back to church." We cringe away from His love and goodness because we don't think we're worthy. The truth is, we're not worthy in and of ourselves. We will never be able to make ourselves worthy of standing before God. We try to clean ourselves up first, like children trying to wash themselves at the sink, and all they do is smear around the dirt. What the child needs is to jump in the shower. That shower is found in the shed blood of Jesus. Only His blood can wash away the things that dirty and defile us.

I've put relationships and my desires above God in the past. I made decisions that cost me life-giving relationships, ministry, reputation, and dignity. It also brought an all-consuming shame I could not shake. I tried to clean myself up before I considered myself worthy to enter God's presence. I tried to be good enough. But like the dirty kid, I ended up smearing around the dirt. In the end, I had to do what 1 John 1:9 (NKJV) says. "If we confess our sins, He is faithful and just to forgive us our sins and to cleanse us from all unrighteousness."

Right standing with God means we can be in His presence without sin-consciousness.

Embracing Forgiveness and Restoration Through Righteousness

As disciples of Jesus, when we realize we've been living in opposition to God's Word and will, we must run to God and ask for forgiveness. He wants to forgive and restore us. He wants to wash us clean and remove our shame so we can live in a close relationship with Him again. When He forgives us, to Him it's as though it never happened. We have a right standing with God, which the Bible calls righteousness, and we can be in His presence without sin-consciousness. We no longer focus on our sin. We focus on Him and His goodness. Our relationship with Him is restored.

God pours out a double portion as we pursue Him, as if this were not enough. He restores what we lost. While many people's minds immediately go to money and wanting a double portion of whatever finances they lost, this restoration is much more than physical wealth. When God restores, He focuses on the spiritual first. Natural things take care of themselves when we seek first God's kingdom and His righteousness. We prosper and are in health even as our soul prospers. If our soul, which is our mind, will, and emotions, are not prospering, then our health and material goods will not prosper either. This is why repentance and the removal of shame are so important to the disciple of Jesus. Until there is a change of heart, there will not be a change of actions. Repentance and the removal of shame bring a change of heart that affects our actions. Only then will we manage the physical things God has given us wisely and under the Holy Spirit's leadership.

Prayer:

Heavenly Father, thank You for teaching me about shame. Thank you for being willing to forgive my sins and remove my shame. I have lived in shame for so long, and I don't want to live this way anymore. Please forgive me for sinning against You, running from You, and believing I deserve to live in shame. Please take this shame and replace it with your peace and joy. I ask mercy and grace to run to You the next time I fail. Thank you again for freeing me. I love you, Daddy God. In Jesus' name, Amen.

Your Turn:

- What is a source of shame you need to get rid of?
- According to the Bible, what is the proper approach to that problem (regarding shame), and what is the recommended course of action?
- Join The Conversation—What's something in this devotion that stuck out to you the most?

Katherine Hutchinson-Hayes
A Practical Guide to Restoring Peace

You will keep in perfect peace those whose minds are
steadfast, because they trust in you.
Isaiah 26:3 (NIV)

I can't count how many times I've found myself on the edge of something meaningful—only to be met with a storm.

For me, this often happens before a major ministry moment, especially when I'm preparing to speak at an event or attend a writers' conference. I know it's where I'm supposed to be. I've prayed over it, prepared for it, and poured myself into it. But like clockwork, chaos seems to meet me at the door.

Navigating Life's Unexpected Challenges and Maintaining Focus

Suddenly, small (or not-so-small) arguments flare up at home, deadlines pile up with work, my body feels weary, and things around me begin to unravel. It's as if the enemy is determined to shake my peace, distract my purpose, and derail my focus.

But over time, I've learned something important: peace doesn't come by accident. It's cultivated—intentionally.

Embracing Peace: A Daily Commitment to Serenity

Peace is a practice. A holy habit. A daily decision to realign my heart with the Prince of Peace when everything else screams for my attention.

What I Do When Peace Feels Out of Reach

I pause and pray—even if it's messy. Sometimes it's a whispered "Help me, Lord" between packing my bags and reprinting my itinerary. God meets us in the whirlwind.

I guard my atmosphere. I turn off the noise and put on worship music, a sermon, or sit in silence with my Bible open. Chaos can't survive where His presence dwells.

I remind myself: attacks don't equal failure. Just because things feel out of control doesn't mean I'm on the wrong path. In fact, it often confirms I'm on the right one.

I breathe and surrender. Control is an illusion. Peace is found in trusting that God goes before me, walks beside me, and carries me when I can't take another step.

Even in the Storm, I've Found Peace

No, things still don't always go perfectly. My luggage has been lost, my flights have been delayed, and my computer and notes have been forgotten. But I've found the profound, soul-restoring truth that peace is not the absence of trouble—it's the presence of God in the middle of it.

When I lean into that truth, I can hear God more clearly, follow His direction, and step fully into what He's called me to do.

Prayer:

Heavenly Father, You are the God of all peace. In the chaos of preparation and the noise of life, still my anxious thoughts. Speak into the storm within me and around me. Help me to be anchored in You, to walk in trust, and to recognize Your presence even when everything feels out of place. Teach me how to restore peace—Your peace—in every moment. In Jesus' name, Amen.

Your Turn:

- What are your biggest peace-stealers right now?
- Are you currently in a season of preparation for something important?
- What is God showing you in this time?
- What small, practical step can you take today to invite God's peace into your space?

Andy Hollifield
The High Cost of Freedom

*And the chief captain answered, With a great sum
obtained I this freedom. And Paul said, But I was
freeborn.*
Acts 22:28 (KJV)

This quote from the Bible, spoken by Paul, a man who was born a Roman citizen and therefore free, but who also understood the value of spiritual freedom, serves as a powerful reminder of the high cost of freedom. We often take our freedom for granted without realizing the cost we have paid for it. Someone paid the price for the liberty we enjoy. In 1944, the Allied forces, including the U.S., invaded northern France. Their mission was to liberate France from Nazi occupation. The official name was "Operation Overlord," but it became known as D-Day. The following statistics are obtained from "The Historic D-Day Invasion: A Turning Point in World War II."[4]

The Historic D-Day Invasion: A Turning Point in World War II

The largest amphibious military operation in history saw 18,000 parachutists drop by dawn, while 6,000 landing craft carried at least 155,000 soldiers to beaches including Gold, Juno, Sword, and Utah. Omaha Beach was especially brutal, with 2,000 Allied casualties. By day's end, over 155,000 Allied troops—Americans, British, and Canadians—had secured Normandy. By June's end, 850,000 men and 150,000 vehicles were in the region, preparing to advance across

Europe. Over 9,000 Allied soldiers were killed or wounded, highlighting the high cost of freedom.

The US only managed to get about twenty-five percent of its supplies to shore, having lost the rest. However, this battle greatly reduced the Germans' capabilities and marked a turning point in the war. The figures vary greatly and will probably remain unknown regarding how many were wounded, missing, taken prisoner, or killed. The numbers even differ on how many were in Normandy by the end of June, ranging from 850,000 to over one million. By August 1944, the Allies had liberated Northern France.

Remembering the Sacrifices of World War II

Today, 9,383 servicemen and four women rest at Normandy's American cemetery above Omaha Beach. Before D-Day, nearly 12,000 had already been lost. In August 1945, the US dropped atomic bombs on Hiroshima and Nagasaki, ending the war. Over fifty million military and civilian lives were lost worldwide since Hitler's 1939 invasion of Poland. Today, 9,383 servicemen and four women rest at Normandy's American cemetery above Omaha Beach. Before D-Day, nearly 12,000 had already been lost. In August 1945, the US dropped atomic bombs on Hiroshima and Nagasaki, ending the war. Over fifty million military and civilian lives were lost worldwide since Hitler's 1939 invasion of Poland.

My point is that many soldiers paid a high price for the freedom we enjoy. Had the Allied forces not been victorious, Germany would have likely taken over the entire world. We should honor the men and women who served in the war. According to the Department of Veterans Affairs, as of 2021, around 200,000 American WWII veterans were still alive. That is down from 620,000 in 2016.

A Selfless Sacrifice

There was a time in history when one man made a selfless sacrifice similar to that of our brave servicemen and women. However, his sacrifice far outweighs anything any of us has ever done for others. Approximately two thousand years ago, a man (fully God and fully human) volunteered to sacrifice his life for the benefit of all mankind. Though rejected, he persisted until his death, even for those who refused to believe him. He could have refused to serve, but gave up his royal seat and served as an ordinary man—a selfless act that continues to inspire us today.

Imagine that! A man set aside his royal crown to fight a battle he could have avoided, for a world full of people who had no regard for his life or the fact that he was willing to sacrifice it in battle.

The Ancient Battle: Lucifer's Rebellion and the Triumph of Good

Oh yes, a great battle had raged long before man inhabited the earth. It began before recorded time, when the archangel Lucifer, along with about a third of the heavenly host, rose in opposition and attempted to overthrow God. Of course, Lucifer and his followers were condemned, expelled, and cast down to hell, prepared for them by God. This victory of good over evil in the spiritual realm gives us hope and reassurance in our battles.

This great man, who was willing to commit to this battle, was none other than Jesus Christ, the Son of God and a part of the Holy Trinity in heaven. He was conceived on earth when the Holy Ghost overshadowed a young Jewish girl. Having chosen to set aside his royal status in Revelation chapter 5, he came into the world as a baby. As an adult, he sacrificed his life, gaining forgiveness for all sins.

After God created the first man, Adam, and his wife, Eve, Lucifer, now known as Satan, approached the woman in the Garden of Eden. He deceived her into believing that disobeying God wouldn't lead to death. God knew this would happen and already had a plan for forgiving man's sin. Christ's willingness to be the ultimate sacrifice would satisfy God's heart and create a pathway for man's forgiveness. Heaven, earth, and the depths below had been searched, but no other perfect man was found suitable to be that sacrifice.

The Choice Between Jesus and Barabbas: A Pivotal Moment in History

The rest is history. Jesus died on the Roman cross for sins he didn't commit, so those who had committed sins could go free. The first was Barabbas, who had been sentenced to death for his part in a revolt against the government. The leader, Pontius Pilate, gave a mob that had assembled against Jesus a choice between him and the criminal Barabbas. The crowd, blinded by hatred and not realizing the will of God was being fulfilled, chose to let Barabbas live and crucify Jesus in his place.

There had been only mock trials, complete with false witnesses against him, senseless beatings, and public shaming. Even as he hung on the cross dying, the crowd and the Roman soldiers united in ridiculing and mocking him. The crowd, still unaware of what they were doing, continued and even stripped him of his clothes, and the soldiers gambled for them. Strange darkness covered the earth from noon until three in the afternoon. As he approached the end of his life, Jesus cried out in a loud voice, praying, "Into thy hands, I commend my spirit." With those words, he surrendered and died. A very thick veil hung in the temple, serving to separate God and humanity because of sin. It was torn from top to bottom at the exact moment Jesus died. These events, the darkness, and the veil had never happened before.

Revelation at the Cross: The Thief's Faith and the Temple's Veil

One of the thieves hanging on the cross beside Jesus believed in Him. Jesus responded by telling the man he would be with Him in Paradise that day. Naturally, this brought the crowd to a fever pitch. Now, He was dead, and the temple's veil had been torn. Some believed in Him that day, and some of the soldiers admitted He was a righteous man. One even confessed that He must be the Son of God.

Heaven's host of angels had to stand idly by during this event. For the first and only time, God turned His back on Jesus. Thirty-three years away from His Father, and this was how it would end. It's not a sad story, however, because, unlike the sacrifices of WWII, this one has a happy ending. Three days after his death, one of his followers, a woman named Mary, found him alive. She came to the tomb early that morning. Jesus instructed his disciples on what to tell them. They had given up everything to follow him.

The Ascension and Promise of Jesus: A Forty-Day Journey

Sometime that day, he ascended to heaven, likely to a celebration like no other. He presented himself and his shed blood to the Father as the ultimate payment for sin. After returning to Earth and meeting with his disciples, Jesus spent forty days instructing them. Many others who had died were seen alive after his resurrection. The government or religious leaders of the day could explain none of this. At the end of the forty days, he went out to a mountain with many of his followers. From there, he ascended back into heaven to his Father, but promised to return for those who believed in him.

Heaven gave its best—the Son of God, who sacrificed his life on the cross to offer forgiveness of sins to everyone willing to believe and accept him. His invitation to believe and receive forgiveness is open to all who choose to accept it. "Greater love hath no man than this, that a man lay down his life for his friends" (John 15:13, KJV).

This sacrifice has been a constant throughout history, from the first soldier to fall in battle to the last. But never has sacrificing one's life for friends meant so much. Freedom, without a doubt, truly comes at a high cost.

Prayer:

Dear Father, help me consider the value of Christ giving his life to give me the freedom found in salvation. Forgive me for taking my freedoms for granted, both spiritual and physical. Please show me how to live gratefully, recognizing the grave sacrifices others have made and continue to make, so that I may enjoy the freedom I have. Amen.

Your Turn:

- What steps can you take to show gratitude for your spiritual and physical freedom?
- Are there things that have held you back? If so, how can you rely on Christ to set you free?

Terrance Niedziela Jr.
Prioritizing God's Authority in Our Lives

*Or do you not know that your body is the temple of the
Holy Spirit who is in you, whom you have from God,
and you are not your own? For you were bought at a
price; therefore glorify God in your body and in your
spirit, which are God's.*
1 Corinthians 6:19-20 (NKJV)

This verse serves as a powerful reminder of our identity as God's possession and the responsibility that comes with it. Recognizing that our lives belong to God compels us to glorify Him in every aspect of our existence. Here are three practical ways to prioritize glorifying God and submit to His authority:

1. **Engage in Daily Prayer and Scripture Reading:**

Establishing a consistent prayer life is vital for nurturing your relationship with God. Set aside dedicated time each day to communicate with Him, sharing your thoughts, concerns, and gratitude. As you pray, invite the Holy Spirit to guide your conversations, helping you discern God's voice amidst the noise of daily life.

Additionally, immerse yourself in Scripture. Reading God's Word not only enriches your understanding of His character and will but also provides wisdom and encouragement for the challenges you face. Consider keeping a journal to record the insights and revelations you receive during this time. This practice will align your mind and heart with God's desires, ultimately helping you recognize areas where you can glorify Him.

2. **Submit to God's Will:**

Actively seeking God's guidance in your decisions is an essential aspect of living under His authority. In every situation, whether it's a major life choice or a simple daily decision, pause and ask yourself, "How does this honor God?" This introspection encourages you to evaluate your motivations and align them with God's purposes.

Practicing submission may require you to let go of personal ambitions or desires that do not align with His will. Surround yourself with individuals who encourage accountability and spiritual growth, as their insights can help you stay on track. Remember, submitting to God's will is a continuous journey, one that requires humility and trust.

3. **Serve Others:**

Serving those around you is a tangible way to glorify God and demonstrate His love in action. Look for opportunities to help others in your community, whether through volunteering, offering support to a friend in need, or simply being a listening ear.

Acts of service reflect Christ's character and remind us that our lives are not solely for our benefit but for the betterment of those around us. Engage in discussions with your community to understand their needs and explore how you can contribute. This not only honors God but also fosters a sense of unity and compassion within the body of Christ.

Prayer:

Heavenly Father, thank You for the incredible gift of Your Holy Spirit and for the authority You hold in my life. I recognize that my body is Your temple, and I desire to glorify You in everything I do. Help me to prioritize prayer, submit to Your will, and serve others selflessly. May my actions reflect Your love and grace in all situations. I ask for guidance as I navigate the challenges of daily life, and I trust that You will lead me closer to You. In Jesus' name, Amen.

Your Turn:

Reflect on your life: In what area do you need to submit more fully to God's authority? Identify one specific action you can take this week to glorify Him in that area. Whether it's dedicating time to prayer, seeking His guidance in a decision, or finding a way to serve others, take that step of faith and witness how God works in your life as you prioritize Him.

Lilka Finely Raphael
Flip the Script:
Turn Us Back to You

Turn us back to You, O Lord, and we will be restored;
Renew our days as of old.
Lamentations 5:21 (NKJV)

Lamentations, by the prophet Jeremiah, reflect on the hardship of Jerusalem following the Israelites' disobedience. During this period, food is scarce, families are shattered, and Israel has succumbed to its enemies. These five chapters contrast the prior beauty and abundance that once flourished in Jerusalem with the consequences of God's wrath. Yet, this book also offers hope. Amid loss and terror, change is possible. It is in the aftermath of destruction that Jeremiah prays for restoration and requests that God "turn us back to You."

The Guiding Hand of the Good Shepherd

Like children prone to wander, we ultimately touch things that burn us and venture into places we shouldn't go. No wonder Jesus Christ is considered the good Shepherd, continually herding us back into safekeeping. As we journey through life and find ourselves in undesirable circumstances, we should look beyond our distress and ask the Lord to turn us back that we may be restored.

Embracing Reconciliation and Restoration Amidst Painful Turns

Though necessary, our turn back can be painful. We may need to turn away from the very things we desire. Our omnipotent and wise

Father knows what is best for us. And everything we want isn't always God's best. Like the Israelites, we often don't recognize our wrongs until tragedy strikes. Mercifully, we don't have to remain among the ruins. Reconciliation and restoration are available.

The Journey of Restoration: Embracing Change and Turning Back to Faith

Still, restoration takes time. We often find ourselves getting into debt or entangled in disastrous relationships over time. It also requires time for God to change our troublesome situations, even as He changes us. Turning back may require a turn of the heart, mind, or both. Sometimes we must come to the end of ourselves before we acknowledge that we need to turn back to God.

If you feel as though ashes surround you, ask God to draw you closer to Him. Flip the script— realizing that hope and mercy abound in dire circumstances. Unlike the Israelites, we have Jesus Christ and the Holy Spirit who intercede, comfort, counsel, heal, and so much more.

Cry out to the Lord and be restored.

Prayer:

Heavenly Father, I come before You with a humble heart, trusting in Your divine wisdom. Help me remember that Your will is always best for my life, even when I do not understand Your plans. Give me the faith to surrender my desires and to seek Your guidance in all that I do. May I find peace in knowing that Your will leads to what is truly good and perfect. Thank you for your love and faithfulness. I trust in Your timing and Your purpose. In Jesus' name, I pray. Amen.

Your turn:

God's word says, Through the Lord's mercies we are not consumed, Because His compassions fail not. They are new every morning; Great is Your faithfulness (Lamentations 3:22-23, NKJV).

After reading this passage, how can you "Flip the Script" by doing the following?

1. Surrender your desires and open your heart to God's guidance today.
2. Let go of your cravings and trust in God's divine plan for your life.
3. Release your will and embrace God's direction—surrender now and find true peace.

Colleen Howard
Upgrades Galore!

*It is for freedom that Christ has set you free. Stand
firm, then, and do not let yourselves be burdened
again by the yoke of slavery.*
Galatians 5:1 (NIV)

I took my first flight when I was three weeks old, and I've logged a lot of airport time since then. Our family always boarded a plane to take summer vacations and weekend getaways. That may sound extravagant, but my dad worked for a major commercial airline. One of the perks was that employees and their immediate families enjoyed free travel. Airlines still offer this, and it's a major bonus for those who work there.

Navigating the World: Our Travel Adventures and Experiences

My husband and I have done our share of traveling through the years. Along the way, we've used various airlines, forged the wilderness of airport security lines, scheduled our ride-shares, and stayed in a variety of hotels.

Despite the many differences between airline carriers, airports, and hotels, the travel industry has one thing in common—it loves offering upgrades for a fee. What do you get with these upgrades? Hotels might offer a better view, a bigger bed, or a larger room. Airlines offer more legroom, first-class, or preferred seating.

The Cost of Comfort: Evaluating Luxury Upgrades

Each of these commodities aims to provide additional comfort, ensuring a more pleasant flight or stay—however, they will also incur a few extra costs. They are one-time offers that serve you for a few hours or a couple of days. Many people love the extra luxury, so they're willing to pay the price. However, if you're anything like me, you may choose to save your money.

In Galatians 5:1 (NIV), God's word tells us, "It is for freedom that Christ has set us free. Stand firm, then, and do not let yourselves be burdened again by a yoke of slavery." Standing firm refers to maintaining one's faith in the face of adverse circumstances. The alternative is to remain enslaved. Therefore, if we don't allow God to set us free, we stay slaves to our sins, worries, and life's cares.

Experience Divine Freedom: A Heavenly Upgrade Awaits You

But what if you heard an announcement offering a no-strings-attached upgrade to increase your freedom, like the promise made in Galatians 5:1? How might you respond? Imagine feeling stuck, discouraged, and alone on life's runway when a booming voice erupts from a loudspeaker, "Ladies and Gentlemen, the Creator of the Universe has a special offer! Would you like to upgrade your life? The Almighty God is offering you freedom from darkness, anxiety, and fear. He will heal your soul and give you rest. Act now, and you'll also receive the unshakeable love of God, the comfort of the Savior, and access to the Global Guidance System of the Holy Spirit. This offer is for everyone—no one is excluded. To receive this generous gift, sign up for the One who runs the ultimate 'Cloud' in the sky to gain 'The Promises of God'. You won't regret it."

The Magnitude of Divine Acts Beyond Earthly Offers

God does BIG things! He parts seas, calms storms, heals the blind, and gives us freedom. However, I'm relatively sure he wouldn't peddle his sacred promises in this manner. After all, this offer is for something more than a penthouse suite, a first-class ticket, or more legroom.

John 10:28 (ESV) God's word says, "I give them eternal life, and they will never perish, and no one will snatch them out of my hand."

Embracing God's Promises: Strength, Compassion, and Guidance

God will never abandon us. He gives us strength to persevere, compassion for those we love, and reminds us that miracles still happen. He teaches us how to guard our hearts and guides us on the path He has prepared for us. These are just a few of His promises.

Unlike the temporary upgrades offered by the travel industry, God's package offers a premium upgrade that's miles above the Gold Medallion status.

Accepting God's Salvation: Mercy, Grace, and Love Through Jesus

When we give our lives to Jesus, we receive His mercy, grace, and love. God's salvation is offered to everyone—all we need to do is open our hearts to receive it. He forgives our sins and forgets them. He hears our prayers and remembers each one.

Take God up on His offer of salvation. Take a deep breath, inhale His grace, and exhale peace. Your life will be changed forever. So, if the Son sets you free, you will be truly free. John 8:36 (NIV).

Prayer:

Dear Jesus, help us stand firm and not fall prey to the burden of sin and slavery. You offer us eternal life and ask us to proclaim your glory to all the world. Give us the courage to share the words that will draw those we love to accept the good news of the gospel. Amen.

Your Turn:

- Who do you love who needs the good news of the gospel?
- How will you pray for them today?
- How can you share the gospel of Jesus with others in your life?
- Where will you start?

Put your trust in the Holy Spirit, and he will lead the way.

Kathy Keenum
An Honorable Commitment

*I will give you a new heart and put a new spirit within
you; I will take the heart of stone out of your flesh and
give you a heart of flesh.*
Ezekiel 36:26 (NKJV)

During my time in the Navy, I learned that it has rules and
standards that must be followed. These are designed to ensure that
departments and divisions operate smoothly. Maintaining loyalty and
camaraderie within the division was essential. The military fosters a
strong, unified group through a clear chain of command and by
adhering to the orders given. The military demands obedience and
commitment.

The Unforeseen Impact of Military Life on Personal Independence

As a sailor, I've often found that a desire to do things my way has
caused tons of trouble. Each time I thought I had a better way, it
usually ended in extra duty or a confrontation with the chief or an
officer. I was neither required nor coerced to join the military. I
volunteered willingly. Coming from a military family, I regarded it as
an honor to serve my country. I had a clear idea of what my life in the
service would entail. However, the impact it ultimately had on my life
was something I did not foresee.

Similarly, I wasn't required or coerced to begin a relationship with the Lord. Much like going into the Navy, I volunteered. I realized I was a sinner and couldn't save myself, but I can only be saved through God's grace and Jesus' sacrifice on the cross to pay for our sins. Commitment and love for the Lord surpass any other commitment in my life, including my dedication to service.

Embracing Faith: Overcoming Stubbornness in My Spiritual Journey

My life was transformed when I became a follower of Christ. What used to be important to me changed. My thoughts and focus began to center on the Lord and the path He had laid out for my life, and I walked in a life committed to following Him in obedience. Still, I have trouble with my stubbornness. There are many times when I resist following God's plan. These failures cause me hardships.

Ezekiel spoke of instilling 'a new spirit within you'—taking out the heart of stone and replacing it with a heart of flesh. Paul echoed this idea in 2 Corinthians 5:17 (ESV): "Therefore, if anyone is in Christ, he is a new creation." The old self has passed away; the new has arrived!

Guarding Against Resistance to Divine Guidance

Unfortunately, there are times when we remain resistant to the Lord—trying to fight against the path He has laid out for us. Our old self tries to take over. However, we must guard against this attack from the enemy.

When we become Christ followers, the Lord instills in our hearts a desire to obey and please Him. A spirit centered around the Lord fills our thoughts. We're transformed. We begin a new way of life—one of obedience and commitment—following the Lord's will. It becomes clear to others that we have experienced a change. As Christ followers, our old, hard hearts are transformed..

Prayer:

Lord, please allow my life to bring glory to you. May my life be an example to others, showing that I am a child of the living God. Grant me the wisdom to follow your will and the strength to stand up for my beliefs. Direct my path so that my life may be sensitive and loving, and not a heart of stone. Amen.

Your Turn:

- Do you have a heart of stone, resisting God's will?
- Has the Lord's grace and love transformed your life?
- Who are you committed to?

<u>Vonyee K. Carrington</u>
It's Okay to be Joyful!

When the Lord restored the fortunes of Zion, we were like those who dream. Then our mouth was filled with laughter, and our tongue with shouts of joy; then they said among the nations, "The Lord has done great things for them."
Psalm 126:1-2 (ESV)

Growing Up Black in Pursuit of the American Dream

I grew up in a middle-class two-parent household in the Midwest and Texas. My sister and I didn't have everything we wanted, but we knew we were loved. My parents worked hard. Like many others, they were chasing the American dream of owning a home. During the pursuit, they still understood that they were raising Black girls in a world that wouldn't always appreciate them.

They made sure my sister and I knew we were cherished, smart, and beautiful. As the oldest, I went with my dad to many places until my sister was born. My mom tells me that when my sister arrived, she took my place as my dad's shadow. She wanted to sit next to him at dinner or behind him in the car. My mom says I took it all in stride. I never doubted that I held a special place in my father's heart.

The Impact of a Father on Building Self-Esteem

The example my father set for me was essential in shaping my healthy self-esteem. Watching him treat others with kindness, respect, and confidence taught me to value myself and believe in my worth. His actions demonstrated what it means to be strong yet compassionate, which has helped me face challenges with resilience and self-assurance.

Fast forward to my first real job after finishing graduate school, where I worked for a church. The visionary pastor was growing a network of churches throughout Virginia, North Carolina, and South Carolina. He intimidated me. I felt the need to anticipate his next move. I didn't do a good job. I was always two steps behind. I felt like I wasn't good enough to meet his expectations.

Overcoming Challenges and Loss of Self-Worth in a Demanding Job

I eventually moved on to a different job where I dealt with demanding and sometimes difficult customers. Some of these customers verbally attacked my gradually diminishing self-esteem. I stayed in this role, and the verbal assaults continued, which slowly worsened my self-esteem even more. By the time I relocated to Florida, I was exhausted and felt like I had lost all sense of worth to anyone.

Three years ago, I landed a position that I truly love. I enjoy the people and the work. The work brings me joy. No customers yelling at me. No scary bosses. Little by little, my self-esteem began to be restored. The Holy Spirit spoke to my heart, "It's okay to be joyful!" I hadn't realized until then that I was holding my breath. I was waiting for something to go wrong in my professional life. I was waiting for someone to start yelling at me. My heart was prepared for a fight, but there wasn't one.

Embracing Restoration: A Journey to Wholeness and Spiritual Renewal

The restoration I've experienced is the process of healing and becoming whole again, especially after hardship, loss, or spiritual distance. It involves reconnecting with God's love, reaffirming faith, and reclaiming a sense of acceptance, peace, and purpose. Restoration is significant because it renews our hope, strengthens our trust in God's plan, and enables us to move forward with renewed strength and clarity. This process often requires patience and openness, but the resulting transformation is deeply fulfilling and sustains us through life's challenges.

Prayer:

Father God, help me begin to see how you are blessing me. As I acknowledge your blessings, may my heart be filled with joy. Restore my trust in you again. Father God, heal the wounds left by past experiences. Let me laugh again with joy. Amen.

Your Turn:

- Have you ever experienced a time when your self-esteem was chipped away? What did you do?
- Did you ever find yourself in the middle of God's blessings, expecting something bad to happen?

Evelyn Collins
Who Tames the Tongue?

*Understand this, my dear brothers and sisters: You
must be quick to listen, slow to speak, and slow to get
angry. Human anger does not produce the
righteousness God desires.*
James 1:19 (NIV)

I often wake up early in the morning to snatch some quiet time before my husband gets up—the perfect time to read, pray, and write. Usually, while I'm sitting in my recliner reading, he walks by, headed to the den. Soon, the sound of the television blares breaks the serenity. When he's awake, our home isn't quiet. Ron likes everything loud—perhaps that comes from his years as a drummer in a local band during high school or his time in the Air Force.

Embracing Solitude and the Art of Listening

I enjoy solitude. Most mornings, weather permitting, my husband sits in front of the garage since the covered entryway is too small. As he listens to his favorite podcasts, he waves to neighbors passing our home. Ron is confident and talkative. He responds instantly, while I hesitate and stumble over my words. When people like him effortlessly engage in conversation, I view their words as self-confident and impactful. I sometimes wonder why—I'm slow to speak.

One day during my quiet time with the Lord, I confessed I wanted to be assertive like my spouse. I saw self-confidence as an asset until

I read James 1:19 in my Bible. Through that scripture, God revealed the virtue of being slow to speak. Being slow to speak has many advantages. It means you are serious and ponder your words. Of course, there are extreme circumstances that warrant an immediate response.

A woman reading her Bible with her husband in the background

The Impact of Hasty Communication in a Fast-Paced World

We live in a fast-paced world that is increasingly active and noisy. Messages fly over the internet. We speak without contemplating our words or considering the viewpoint of others. It is effortless to respond without giving it a thought. We write words we'd never say face-to-face. Our careless words create misunderstandings. We release words, both spoken and written, that we can't take back.

What are the benefits of using restraint with our words?

1. We speak life.

According to James, chapter 3, our tongues are evil and able to destroy our entire body. We speak both life and death with our tongues. Our tongues reveal the true condition of our hearts. Only the Spirit of God can control our tongues. It is an impossible feat for us alone; the Holy Spirit is our helper, and He strengthens us.

2. We receive discernment.

When we listen and are slow to speak, we are waiting for guidance from the Holy Spirit. He reveals Himself by bringing relevant scriptures to our minds. Leaning into the Spirit while listening transforms hearts. Our stony hearts become a pliable vessel. A lack of self-confidence becomes certainty in and dependence upon God. Faith grows. God gives us discernment when we are open to receiving it. We recognize the still whisper from His Holy Spirit.

3. We have a circle of influence.

Although most of us are not paid social media influencers, each of us has a circle of influence within our community. Our influence is good or bad. Listening and understanding are important components of any conversation. When we listen well and focus on the other person's comments, we become less concerned with our responses. If we are Christians who are skilled listeners, our words are purposeful and seasoned with salt. Since our words carry weight and can change the course of another person's life, we choose our words wisely.

4. We are trustworthy witnesses to God's love.

When we are slow to speak, it helps us avoid hasty decisions and commitments. Once we agree to something, we are committed to it. There is an understanding that we will follow through with our commitment. Our actions become more important than our words. Failure to do what we say harms relationships and our witness for Christ. Others no longer consider us trustworthy. Our word is our promise, so we fulfill our agreements.

God is transforming how I speak. Although my nature is to be slow to speak, God uses His Word to show me that I hesitate because of the fear of people. Now my delayed speech is to honor God with the words I speak. The Bible says it this way in Colossians 4:6 (NIV): "Let your conversation be always full of grace, seasoned with salt, so that you may know how to answer everyone."

Prayer:

Father God, thank you for revealing to me the importance of being slow to speak. I desire to honor you by controlling my tongue. It's impossible without your help. Please give me words of life and restoration to speak over others. In Jesus' name I pray, Amen!

Your Turn:

- How important are words to you?
- Do you struggle with taming your tongue?
- What helps you control your words?
- How can you practice being slow to speak?

Crystal Johnson
From Ashes to Flesh:
When God Softens a Hardened Heart

*I will give you a new heart and put a new spirit within
you; I will take the heart of stone out of your flesh and
give you a heart of flesh.*
Ezekiel 36:26 (NKJV)

When Life Hardens the Heart

There was a time in my life when I didn't recognize who I was
becoming. Disappointments, betrayals, and grief piled up silently, like
layers of sediment hardening over my soul. Without realizing it, I
began living a guarded life. My prayers became robotic. My joy felt
distant. Even love, once so natural to offer, became difficult to extend.
Somewhere along the way, I had let pain build walls that even God's
light struggled to penetrate.

Then came the fire. Not figuratively, but literally. I awoke one
morning to a video that left me speechless. My childhood home, the
one filled with echoes of my mother's laughter, late-night prayers, and
warm memories, was engulfed in flames. Watching it burn felt like
losing her all over again. Though I no longer lived there, my siblings
and I still owned it, and that home represented our roots, our
beginnings, our story. Losing it felt like the last physical connection
to a woman who shaped so much of my faith and identity.

The Moment God Met Me

The grief from that fire mixed with all the other grief I had stuffed down the years. I stood at the window one evening, staring out blankly, numb to everything around me. I had just gotten off the phone with a friend who had pointed out how cold I'd become, how guarded and distant I sounded even in everyday conversation. Her words stung, but they were true.

Later that night, I opened my Bible and read the verse that would change me: "I will give you a new heart and put a new spirit within you…" (Ezekiel 36:26, NKJV). Tears came swiftly. It felt like a whisper from Heaven straight to my weary soul. I didn't need to fix myself. I needed God to do heart surgery. I needed Him to replace the bitterness, the guardedness, the numbness with flesh. With tenderness. With Spirit. So, I whispered a simple prayer: *Lord, I don't want this hardened heart anymore. Please give me a new one.*

Beauty From Ashes

The healing didn't happen overnight. God peeled back the layers slowly, through his word, through worship, through the kindness of others, and yes, even through more pain. He used Isaiah 43:19 (NKJV) to speak of hope: "Behold, I will do a new thing… I will even make a road in the wilderness and rivers in the desert." And Psalm 51:10 (NKJV) became my anthem: "Create in me a clean heart, O God, and renew a steadfast spirit within me."

The burning down of my childhood home became symbolic of something greater—God was clearing out the old. Not just wood and brick, but places in my spirit that had grown too attached to the past.

Places that needed to be surrendered. Isaiah 61:3 (NKJV) promises that God gives us "beauty for ashes, the oil of joy for mourning." And that's exactly what he did. He reminded me that what I lost in form, I had not lost in spirit. That his presence would be my new dwelling place. And that my mother's legacy wasn't lost in the fire; it lived on in me.

He Makes All Things New

Even now, I still carry the scars of specific seasons. They don't ache the way they used to. My heart beats softer now, more responsive to God's leading, more open to love, more grounded in eternal perspective. I no longer feel stuck in grief. I feel carried by grace. Jesus said in Revelation 21:5 (NKJV), "Behold, I make all things new." He meant it, even when your heart has grown cold, even when you feel numb, even when all you can see are ashes.

Can You Relate?

If you find yourself walking through a season of loss, or if your heart has quietly hardened from years of pain or disappointment, know this:

- God still gives new hearts.
- You don't have to pretend to be okay.
- You don't have to hold it all together.

All he asks is that you open the door. Let him in. Let him work. And watch how he replaces stone with flesh, sorrow with joy, and ashes with beauty.

Prayer:

Father, I come to you with the pieces of my heart, broken, tired, and in need of you. Take away this heart of stone and give me a heart of flesh. Soften the places that life has hardened. Heal what grief has wounded. Make me tender again to your voice, your spirit, and your love. I believe you are doing a new thing in me, and I receive it today with faith. In Jesus' name, Amen.

Your Turn:

- Has there been a time when you sensed your heart growing hard?
- How did God begin to soften it?

Colleen Howard
Surrender, Dorothy!

*I am saying this for your own good, not to restrict
you, but that you may live in a right way in undivided
devotion to the Lord.*
1 Corinthians 7:35 (NIV)

I love Jesus. He is my Savior, redeemer, and keeper of my heart. I love my husband, family, and friends. I love to read. I love words, and I love the movies.

Seriously, I really love movies. I quote them; I know weird, random movie facts, and I even took cinema classes in college. Old movies, new movies, funny, dramatic, poignant, and character-driven, I'm a sucker for a well-written film. Give me a good movie with clever dialogue, and bring on the popcorn.

The Timeless Appeal of "The Wizard of Oz": A Journey into Nostalgia

I recently watched a segment of CBS Sunday Morning News, and according to CBS, the Library of Congress reports that the most-watched movie of all time is the 1939 film The Wizard of Oz, based on Frank L. Baum's Oz book series.[5] This captured my attention and led me down a nostalgic trail into the world of Oz.

I first saw the film when I was about seven years old and watched it year after year, each time it was televised. Spoiler alert—those flying monkeys are still terrifying.

The film begins with young Dorothy being swept up by a tornado and landing in the mysterious Land of Oz. Not fully understanding how this happened, all she wants to do is go home.

The Journey to the Wizard of Oz: Allies and Adversaries

Alone and confused, Dorothy is told by Glinda, the Good Witch, that the wizard will help. If she follows the yellow brick road, it will take her directly to the Wizard. Along the way, she meets three friends, and together, they journey down the yellow brick road to find the Wizard of Oz. But it wouldn't be a magnificent film without a villain. The clever enemy who's out to get the fearless foursome is none other than the Wicked Witch of the West.

Dorothy and her friends are led to believe the Wizard will explain everything. A familiar line in the film is, "The great and powerful Oz has got matters all in hand."

But the Wicked Witch plans to keep Dorothy from the Wizard. Her message is grim and written across the sky in capital letters: "SURRENDER, DOROTHY!"

So, what is Dorothy's trek down the yellow brick road doing in this devotion?

With every passing year, I see God's word in action everywhere I turn. As I watched the CBS News segment, I saw a profound life lesson woven through the story of the Wizard of Oz.

According to 1 Corinthians 7:35, God wants us to surrender all to Him and give Him our undivided devotion. He explains, it's not to limit us, but to help us serve the Lord without distraction.

The Transformative Power of Surrendering to Faith

What does surrender require of us? It requires giving God our thoughts and actions. Surrendering all to serve Christ changes how we see the world and the way we live.

Just like Dorothy, we sometimes want to (metaphorically) go home. Perhaps we want to turn back the clock, have one more visit with a loved one who has passed, or simply have a do-over of yesterday. However, the answer is found in the word surrender.

The current culture has attached a slew of negative connotations to the word surrender. The Dictionary online describes surrender as "giving up possessions, surrendering to someone, or abandoning hope."[6]

But God views surrender as a necessary part of our faith walk. When we let God saturate our lives, He directs our paths and shapes our choices. God's Word tells us to demolish arguments and every lofty opinion raised against the knowledge of God, and take every thought captive to obey Christ. (2 Corinthians 10:5, ESV)

Giving in to God is an act of obedience. When we surrender to the Savior, He gives us the freedom to walk confidently in faith and pray bold prayers. Surrender to the Holy One who placed the stars in the sky. "That according to the riches of his glory, he may grant you to be strengthened with power through his Spirit in your inner being" (Ephesians 3:16, ESV).

Prayer:

Dear Jesus, give us the courage to surrender all to you freely. You are the God who keeps the planets in orbit; even so, you know every detail of our lives. As we stand before you, help us realize you are bigger than big and closer than close. Thank you for calling us out of darkness into your marvelous light. Amen.

Your Turn:

Surrender is trusting God more than yourself. Recall a time when you surrendered something to God. Reflect on the details and how He guided your choices. Is there something in your life today that God is urging you to surrender? Ask Him for the courage to let go of the past and step into a new place of trust in your faith walk.

DiAnn Mills
Don't Use Skim Milk in God's Recipe for Life

I have come that they may have life, and have it to the fullness of God's love. Explore the wisdom of your God-time without an eye on the time.
John 10:10 (NIV)

Nourish Your Spirit—Embracing the Fullness of Life: Nourishment for Body and Spirit

Whole milk is packed with essential nutrients that our bodies need, just as a robust spiritual life provides the richness and fullness of life that Jesus offers, encouraging us to seek a deep and authentic relationship with Him rather than settling for superficial shortcuts.

In today's world, many of us are constantly seeking shortcuts in various aspects of our lives. Whether it's in our diets, our work, or our spiritual journeys, the appeal of the easy way out can be tempting. But when it comes to living a fulfilling and purposeful life, there are no substitutes for the real thing. Just like we wouldn't want to use skim milk in a savory, flavorful recipe, we shouldn't skimp on the godly ingredients that truly nourish our souls.

I understand that not everyone can enjoy dairy. For those who are lactose intolerant, think of this analogy in terms of your favorite milk alternatives—like almond milk, oat milk, or soy milk. The principle remains the same: opting for the full-fat versions of these alternatives can represent embracing the richness and depth of a full life, while the lighter versions might symbolize taking shortcuts. How can we avoid shortcuts for a rich, full life with God?

Embrace the Whole Experience

Consider the taste difference between whole milk, which provides a richer, creamier taste, and skim milk. Our mouths water! Imagine embracing the entirety of life's experiences—both the good and the challenging—to create a fuller, more satisfying journey. By facing obstacles and overcoming hardships, we grow and deepen our faith.

Don't Settle for Less Embrace the Fullness: Avoiding Shortcuts in Health and Spirituality

In our "take the shortcut" view of life, we often settle for less than what we truly need. Skim milk might seem like a healthier choice because it has less fat, but it also lacks the richness and nutrients of whole milk. Similarly, in our spiritual lives, we shouldn't settle for superficial practices. Dive deep into prayer, study the Scriptures, and engage in meaningful community to experience the fullness of God's love. Explore the wisdom of your God-time without an eye on the time.

Nourish Your Spirit

Whole milk is packed with essential nutrients that our bodies need, just as a robust spiritual life provides the sustenance our souls crave. Regular worship, fellowship with other believers, Bible study, and acts of volunteer service are vital to a spiritually nourishing life.

Authenticity Over Convenience

In a world that often skips over authenticity, remember that true fulfillment comes from being genuine and wholehearted in our pursuits. Just as you wouldn't want to bake a cake with skim milk and miss out on its full flavor, we don't want to shortchange our relationship with God by taking the easiest path to spiritual growth. Experiencing and processing pain, rather than ignoring it, fosters stronger spiritual growth.

Cultivating a Deep Relationship with God Through Pursuing Patience and Persistence

Good things take time. We get distracted—Satan's best tool for pulling us away from God. We long to create a rich, delicious dish. But it requires patience and attention to detail, and so does pursuing a deep and meaningful relationship with God. Don't rush through quiet times and Bible study to check off a box. When we invest our hearts in the relationship that matters for eternity, we receive blessings.

Trust in God's Recipe

God has a perfect plan for each of us, and His recipe is designed to grow us more in the likeness of Jesus. Trust in His guidance, even when the process seems slow or challenging. Just as a master chef knows the right ingredients and techniques to create a masterpiece, God knows what we need to become the best versions of ourselves.

Living a life of faith isn't about taking shortcuts or settling for less. It's about embracing the fullness of God's love and the richness of His plan for us. So, don't use skim milk in God's recipe for your life. Choose the whole, nourishing experience that will lead to true fulfillment and joy.

What tip can you give for using richness in God's recipe for life?

Prayer:

God, thank you for the richness of your love and the fullness you invite us to experience. Help us to avoid shortcuts in our spiritual lives and to embrace the whole journey You have set before us. Teach us to seek deep connection with You through prayer, Your Word, and community. Give us patience and persistence as we grow in faith, trusting Your perfect plan. May we choose the full, nourishing life with You over superficial shortcuts. Strengthen us to nourish our spirits and to pursue authenticity in all we do. Thank You for Your grace and guidance along the way. In Jesus' name, we pray. Amen.

Your Turn:

- In what areas of your life might you be tempted to take shortcuts spiritually? What changes could you make to seek a fuller, more nourishing relationship with God?
- How can embracing the full experience of life—both challenges and blessings—deepen your faith?
- Are there practices in your spiritual routine that need to be "full-fat" to better nourish your soul?
- What patience or persistence do you need to cultivate to grow closer to God?

- How can you encourage others to pursue authenticity and fullness in their spiritual journeys?

<u>Andy Hollifield</u>
Don't Pray Your Way Out Of God's Blessings

For I know the thoughts that I think toward
you saith the LORD, thoughts of peace, and not of
evil, to give you an expected end.
Jeremiah 29:11 (KJV)

I'm glad God knows the "expected end" he has for me. This is one of my favorite days of the year. Many times throughout my life, I wondered if my end would come sooner rather than later. This was especially true back in 1983. As cocky as I was, on the exact day I turned 18 ½, I underwent a kidney transplant that would not only save my life, but in many ways, dictate how I lived it. I was a scared, confused kid who had, nine months earlier, been forced to grow up instantly and way too fast. October 6th is the 42nd anniversary of the second-greatest event in my life: that surgery. The first was when the Lord saved my soul on October 2nd, 1973. You may think my wedding and the birth of my son should rank ahead of the surgery, but without it, those two would've probably never happened. I've had a few bone issues and three joint replacements, but I'll take them. For the life God has given me, by way of my older brother Jim, joint replacements are a small price to pay.

Trusting in God's Plan and Peace Through Life's Uncertainties

It's comforting to know that in the verse above, God has "an expected end" for his children. It's expected because he's the one who decides it for each of us. Hebrews 9:27 says we each have an appointment with death, and that is one appointment we'll keep. Though my life may have turned out differently from what I had planned, I'm glad God already knew the outcome. He planned it, and none of my life events have caught him off guard. He has never wrung his hands, wondering what he was going to do next. The verse above said he has thoughts of peace toward me, and not of evil. Romans 8:28 promises that all things, both good and bad, work together for our long-term benefit. At that time, I couldn't see that, and didn't like it, but it was my life, and I had to live it. I'm thankful his thoughts toward me were thoughts of peace because peace was the last thing on my mind back then. My whole world had been turned upside down and spinning off its axis, in my opinion.

Little did I know then that forty-two years later, I would be sitting at a computer writing and bragging about how good God has been to me. I spent all my life planning to be an over-the-road trucker. The only thing I wrote was country songs. But God, who knew me before he created me in my mother's womb, knew my life story from before the womb to beyond the tomb. There has never been a second of my life that has surprised him or sent him into a panic. Psalms 139 is a beautiful chapter about how well God knows us and how precious his thoughts toward us are.

Trusting God's Plan: Embracing the Unknown Future

I kind of wonder if, back in those days, God ever looked at me and thought, boy, if you only knew what I have ahead for you, you wouldn't grumble and worry about things you can't do anything about. I wonder if he got anxious when I thought my life was over, and thought, if you only knew that in 2016, I would have you start writing on Facebook to encourage people every day. You'll reach more people through your writing than you ever would on your own. I'll have you writing books to teach youth and encourage saints. I wonder if God ever looks at me in frustration because I fail to trust him as I should.

I didn't want to bore you with details about my life and surgery. That's why I wrote this in a way to give God his glory. Even when I didn't know what he was doing, he did. When I was backsliding, he didn't love me any less, even though I brought reproach on his name. When I fail and come short of his glory, he still loves me like I was his only child.

Trusting God's Plan Through Life's Trials

Have you ever given thought to the drastic situations in your life? Those times when you were at your wits' end, but God just smiled and kept working on your case, already knowing the outcome. Too often, we're prone to advise God on his job or tell him our opinion. How many times have we prayed and asked God to take us out of a situation? Thereby, we missed the blessing and joy he already had for us if we stuck it out to the end and trusted him. The trials we endure aren't sent to destroy us, but to mold us into what God wants us to be.

Whatever you're facing right now, accept it and ask God for more grace to get through it. He might be merciful and deliver you right now, but you may also be praying your way out of a blessing. It's a joyous time when you come through a trial and are restored to God's fellowship because he proved Himself faithful even though you sometimes weren't.

Prayer:

Lord help us to remember Romans 8:26 (KJV) where Paul says, "Likewise the Spirit also helpeth our infirmities: for we know not what we should pray for as we ought: but the Spirit itself maketh intercession for us with groanings which cannot be uttered." Help us to be mindful that your Holy Ghost is always before your throne interceding on our behalf. Give us the grace we need to endure hardship as good soldiers (2 Timothy 2:3), realizing that rewards await us in heaven if we put our trust in you for all things. Let us always be mindful of those who watch our lives, especially in trying times, to see if our faith remains intact or if we display a weak God who cannot deliver us in times of difficulty. Help me always be a display of your grace and mercy, even in the most heartbreaking situations I may face. Amen.

Your Turn:

- Have you ever given thought to the drastic situations in your life? Those times when you were at your wit's end, but God just smiled and kept working on your case, already knowing the outcome.

- Have you ever been guilty of trying to tell God how to do his job and tell him what you needed, although he already knows?
- Have you ever prayed, asking God to fix your situation by delivering you from it?

Lilka Finely Raphael
Rest and Restoration

*Do not conform to the pattern of this world but be
transformed by the renewing of your mind. Then you
will be able to test and approve what God's will is—
his good, pleasing and perfect will.*
Romans 12:2 (NIV)

There are times in life when we feel like we're losing our minds.
Breaking news and nonstop notifications update us constantly
regarding humanity's decline. Chasing success by society's standards
only leaves us frustrated and mentally exhausted. Thankfully, our
Father instructs us how to regain our sanity and enjoy the abundant
lives He desires for us.

Finding Peace and Guidance Through God's Word

God's word comforts our souls and offers peace that quiets the
chatter that distracts from what is true. We are commanded not to yield
to the world but to instead submit to the word. Romans 12:2 infers that
this must be a continual process if we are to overcome our trials and
discern God's perfect will.

The renewal we require can be found through prayer and
devotions. It is also manifested by worship. Even sitting still long
enough to seek the Lord with an eager ear eventually yields revelation.
No matter the method, it is our earnest thirst for God, not earthly
pleasures, that ultimately transforms us. This transformation provides
the rest and restoration we need to sustain us through trying times.

Winning the Inner Battle Through Spiritual Renewal

The battles we fight originate in the mind. Continual renewal grants us the wisdom to win the war. We will never recognize or comprehend our purpose or realize our dreams if our thoughts remain chaotic and unaligned with scripture. The refreshing available only from our Father directs us toward obedience to heed the Spirit, provides vision for the future, and empowers us to maximize our talents.

Each day requires its own allotment of grace, guidance, and strength from the Lord. It is God's restoration that shifts our thoughts from current circumstances toward His faithful promises. As a result, we can regain our peace, reaffirm our faith, and revive our hope regardless of breaking headlines. When we reset our minds through prayer, devotion, worship, and study, we reduce our capacity for pride, greed, lust, and envy. Dedicating time to the Lord and submitting ourselves to His plans enables us to think on those things that are noble, pure, lovely, and praiseworthy.

Embracing Rest to Fulfill God's Will

When in doubt, clear it out—worldly desires, anxiety, and fear. Embrace the rest and restoration that transforms us into beacons on a hill—followers of Christ determined to fulfill God's will.

"Turn my eyes away from vanity [all those worldly, meaningless things that distract—let Your priorities be mine] And restore me [with renewed energy] in Your ways" (Psalm 119:37, AMP).

Prayer:

Heavenly Father, thank You for the rest and restoration You offer through Your Word, prayer, and worship. I acknowledge that my mind can become overwhelmed by the chaos of the world and the false promises of earthly success. I seek Your wisdom to renew my thoughts, to align them with Your truth, and to find peace amid the noise. Help me to prioritize You daily, to eagerly seek Your presence, and to trust in Your promises. Restore my soul, renew my mind, and empower me to reflect Your love and light in all I do. Grant me the strength to resist worldly distractions and the humility to continually surrender to Your will. In Jesus' name, I pray. Amen.

Your Turn:

- What worldly distractions tend to steal your peace and focus?
- How can you intentionally carve out time each day for prayer, worship, or Bible study?
- In what areas of your life do you need renewal and restoration?
- How can you practice renewing your mind throughout the day?
- What specific steps can you take to shift your thoughts from worry and chaos to trust in God's promises?

Remember, restoration is ongoing—lean into His grace and truth.

Colleen Howard
Bumpy Beginnings

If I must boast, I will boast of the things that show my weakness.
2 Corinthians 11:30 (ESV)

My first year as a classroom teacher was disastrous. I was overwhelmed by doubt, negative feelings, and self-critical thoughts. Every day, I thought, "Someone's going to walk in here and find out I have no idea what I'm doing!" My self-assessment revealed the real issue—a lack of experience, not a lack of education. The move from teaching small groups to a large class didn't go smoothly. I made many mistakes when I transitioned from a special needs setting to a general fifth-grade classroom.

Regrouping and Starting Anew: A Classroom Transformation

One day, overcome by a conviction to regroup, I instructed the students to gather with me in a circle on the floor. Huddled together, I confessed that I'd caused them to have gotten off to a bumpy beginning. From there, I shared changes I planned to implement in classroom management and explained how those adjustments would affect them. They asked questions, I gave answers, and we agreed to start over.

This wasn't an easy task, and the transition of the classroom's climate took considerable time. I realized there's always something more to learn, and coming clean about your mistakes is humbling, but effective.

However, that didn't eliminate the persistent doubt about my teaching skills. I was bombarded with nagging thoughts of someone walking into the classroom and discovering I was unqualified.

Understanding Imposter Syndrome: The Doubt That Challenges Competence

Psychologists have given this phenomenon the name Impostor Syndrome, which sows seeds of doubt in the minds of qualified people. This syndrome is characterized by persistent self-doubt and fear of being exposed as a fraud, despite evidence of one's competence.

God used this experience to encourage me to continue learning more about my chosen profession. This prompted me to return to school to learn more. My program of study turned out to be an exhilarating, exhausting two years, but worth every moment.

Embracing Weakness to Highlight Divine Strength

God is aware that we struggle and we're not perfect—He created us. But our weaknesses should bring God's strength to the forefront. His word tells us that we should boast about our weaknesses, which shines a light on His strength. Sometimes we focus more on our weaknesses than our successes. Yet, it's vital to flip the script by sharing our struggles and asking for God's help.

It's just as important to acknowledge our strengths and wins. When we do this, He can and will restore us and help us as we depend on Him and as we remain grateful for our gifts.

Prayer:

Dear God, I come before You, acknowledging our imperfections and the weaknesses that we often carry. Thank you for understanding us completely, even in our struggles. Help us to embrace our flaws and to see them as opportunities to showcase Your strength and power in our lives. Guide us to boast in our weaknesses, as Your word teaches us, so that Your light may shine brightly through us. May we not dwell solely on our shortcomings, but also recognize and celebrate our achievements and victories that come from You. Lord, remind us to share our struggles with others and to seek Your assistance in times of need. As we lean on You, may we feel Your restoration and grace. We are grateful for the blessings You have bestowed upon us, and we thank You for the strength You provide. In your holy name, we pray, Amen.

Your Turn:

Imposter syndrome is a creepy feeling, filling us with fear that someone will find out we don't know what we're doing.

- Have you ever felt like an imposter?
- When was that, and why did you think this way?
- How can you depend more on God to help you through feelings of inadequacy?
- In what areas do you flourish?
- How can you continue to nurture your gifts?

Andy Hollifield
Don't Forget The Miracles

For they considered not the miracle of the loaves,
for their heart was hardened.
Mark 6:52 (KJV)

Reflecting on the miracles of Jesus, we see that many times in the bible hearts can sometimes remain hardened despite witnessing divine power firsthand. From the woman healed by her faith to the raising of Jairus's daughter, and even the feeding of over five thousand, each miracle was a testament to God's power and compassion. Yet, even the disciples, after witnessing these events, forgot His works, and their hearts grew callous.

Remembering God's Miracles: A Call to Deepen Faith and Gratitude

How often do we forget God's miracles in our lives? Surviving accidents, healing our loved ones, or experiencing sudden breakthroughs—these are undeniable acts of God. Let us not allow our hearts to become hardened by forgetfulness. Instead, cherish and remember God's wondrous deeds, for they deepen our faith and keep us rooted in gratitude. Stay vigilant and never underestimate the power of our miraculous God.

Recognizing God's Ongoing Miracles Amidst Spiritual Hardening

Sometimes, after witnessing God's wondrous works, we too can become inattentive or even hardened to His ongoing miracles in our lives. The Bible reminds us in Mark 6:52 (KJV), "For they considered not the miracle of the loaves: for their heart was hardened." The disciples had seen Jesus perform incredible miracles—healing the sick, calming storms, and feeding thousands—and yet, moments later, they forgot those miracles and began to doubt.

Recognizing the Miracles in Our Lives

Think about the miracles you've witnessed in your life: surviving dangerous accidents, miraculous recoveries, unanswered prayers that were eventually answered, or moments of unexpected provision. These are God's undeniable works, personally performed for us. They are beyond explanation and stretch beyond our understanding.

Remembering God's Ongoing Miracles Amid Life's Challenges

It's easy to forget these blessings or take them for granted, especially when life's challenges threaten to discourage us. But remember—our God is still working, still performing miracles, even now.

Prayer:

Heavenly Father, thank You for the countless miracles You've performed in my life. Help me, Lord, to remember Your works, to see Your hand in every blessing, and to keep my heart soft and receptive. Forgive me if I have become hardened or forgetful. Renew my spirit and help me to trust You more fully. May I never forget Your miracles, big or small, and always walk in faith and gratitude. In Jesus' name, I pray. Amen.

Your Turn:

- Can you recall a miracle God has done in your life?
- What are some steps you can take to consistently remind yourself of the amazing things God has done for you and others?
- How do you think staying grateful will affect you and those in your circle?

Ken Howard
Crossing the Red Sea to Our Promised Land

*In their hearts humans plan their course, but
the Lord establishes their steps.
Proverbs 16:9 (NIV)*

What I'm about to share tonight is nothing new to any of us in this room. We've all faced hardships, challenges, and adversity over the course of our lives, but if you can glean anything from our recent experience to help you in your walk as followers of Christ, then I'm honored to share our story.

The question begs to be asked: Why the move? So let me begin by setting the stage.

Our journey began about 6 months ago in March. We had been living in a two-story, tri-level home with multiple sets of steps for 31 years and had been talking about moving to a single-level home for years.

There were two reasons in my mind for this action:
1. Colleen has fallen twice (non-stair-related) and has broken her knee in one incident, and then she broke her hip in a second, yet separate incident. I thought it best we avoid any potential future injuries from slips, trips, and falls down those stairs.
2. At my age, I know my days are numbered. Anything can happen, so in the unlikely event that something should happen

to me, my heart's desire was and is to protect Colleen by providing her with a new home, mortgage-free free so she has one less thing to worry about for the rest of her life without me.

After much prayer, we decided to "pull the trigger" on our journey to a new home this year and trust God for His guidance and provisions.

Immediately, our hot water tank had other plans and decided to leak, causing water damage to adjoining walls and carpet, and delaying our house from getting on the market for a month. In addition, we had to deal with all the stress of working with insurance and multiple contractors for the repair work. Already, adversity was setting in!

In the meantime, we continued our search for a new home with our realtor for about 2 months until we found the house we believed God was directing us to.

Despite the economy, the slow housing market, and rising interest rates, we continued to seek guidance and to trust God through our daily morning quiet times and devotional readings. That never stopped.

Over the next couple of months, we had very little traffic on our old house, even after we reduced the price by $25K. So, we decided to reduce the price by an additional $30k, below the market comps, to generate some interest, and did we stir the pot! People slowly began to inquire about our house.

There were the chicken coop people, the Cirque du Soleil people from Nebraska, and then there were the "Low Ballers."

The "Low Ballers" were unique (not that the chicken coop people or Cirque du Soleil folks were not "unique"), but they showed interest in our house, not once, not twice, but three times, and eventually placed a bid on the house. But in the end, they bailed. Our optimism hit an all-time low—the bottom fell out—our hearts sank.

By now, we had been on a torturous mental, spiritual, and physical roller coaster of a ride. We were exhausted! And the closing of our new house was edging ever closer, and we had no buyers for our old house. Our faith was starting to wane. Did we misunderstand God? Did we do the wrong thing? Why is God delaying his promised rescue and provisions? Why are we in this perceived financial mess?

Two things were going on behind the scenes.

1. God was testing our faith. You may recall Peter said to Jesus before his denial, "Even if I must die with you, I will not deny you!". His intentions were good. We also share Peter's sentiment and good intentions by saying things like, "Lord, no matter what happens in our situation, we will follow you and trust your timing" until we're in the deep trenches of our circumstances. Day after day, week after week, month after month, relief is nowhere to be found, and our closing date is fast approaching! Despair and fear begin to set in, and one faces adversity head-on. There's no escape. It's got a firm grip on us. This is a harsh reality.

2. Guess who also knows and sees our dilemma—yeah, our adversary, the devil, the father of lies—Satan. The one who comes to kill, steal, and destroy the saints. He begins his attack,

subtly, on tiptoe, whispering in your ear, replacing your thoughts of bold faith with doubt. "So, where is your God? Why do you continue to place your faith and trust in a God that cannot be found to rescue you? If this is the house that even God can't sell, then give up!"

Wait a minute, are we talking about the same God of Israel? The God of Abraham, Isaac, and Jacob? The God who created the universe, the heavens, the earth, and all that's in them? The God who set the sun, the moon, and hung the stars in place, and calls each by name? Our Jehovah Jireh, the Lord is my provider? Are we talking about that God?

Just when I thought my faith was hanging by a thread, Colleen shared a devotional with me that she had just read that morning called "Connecting the Dots", by Joel and Jonathan Malm. They talk about turning points that can create lots of anxiety, fear, worry, and concern. The only way to conquer those feelings is to recognize them for what they are, fear, then move forward into the unknown with courage. We have to face our fears!

That was my turning point. I told Colleen, we're moving forward. We're moving forward and we're not looking back. We will stand on the word of God and honor Him by trusting His timing in our bleak circumstances. I picked up the phone and scheduled the movers, then called SRP, the City of Mesa, Southwest Gas, COX, and our Home Security—we're moving!

That week, we had more interested parties look at our house than we had in the previous five months. One of those parties placed a bid on our home. Their bid was more than what the "Low Ballers" had offered. Is God good or what?

Finally, just a day or two before the closing on our new house, our lender and title companies literally jumped through hoops to approve our loan, and we moved into our new home on the expected closing day. The party that bought our old house had their financing approved as well, and they closed earlier than expected and moved into their new home.

In the end, God's ultimate planning and timing were perfect. A win-win situation for everyone. He faithfully navigated us through our "Red Sea" of adversity into our Promised Land, a new home. Praise be to God!

Three takeaways from our story:

1. My timing and planning may not be fully aligned with God's. Proverbs 16:9 (NIV) says, "We can make our plans, but the Lord determines our steps."

2. Delay is not necessarily Denial, but a time of preparing us for His promise and trusting in His process to get there for His glory and our good. He's building upon our confidence and faith in Him.

3. Fear of the unknown induces paralysis. This is Satan's plan, to throw us off course, like a deer in the headlights! Avoid getting stuck here. Act and move forward. God sees and will honor

your actions as a step of bold faith in Him. We're called to walk boldly by faith, not by sight (or fear, for that matter).

Prayer:

Lord, I release every worry, every plan, and every burden into Your hands. Where I have tried to control, help me surrender. Where I have held on tightly, help me trust You fully. Take the lead in my life, guide my steps, and calm my spirit. Teach me to rest in Your wisdom, rely on Your strength, and believe that Your way is always better than mine. I give it all to You, Lord. Have Your way in me. Amen.

Your Turn:

Take a moment to pause and reflect. Where in your life are you still trying to hold the reins? Is it a relationship, a fear, a dream, or a burden you've carried for too long?

Ask yourself:

- What would it look like if I truly let God take control in this area?
- What am I afraid will happen if I surrender?
- What might God be inviting me to release today?

Write your thoughts, your worries, and your hopes. Then offer them to God—open-handed and trusting—believing that He can carry what you cannot.

Shai Johnson
Letting Go and Looking Forward

Forget the former things; do not dwell on the past.
See, I am doing a new thing!
Isaiah 43:18-19 (NIV)

Depression has been a long companion of mine, an invisible burden that's weighed on me for as long as I can remember. It isn't something I can just shake off, and it's not always easy for others to understand. It's a constant battle, one that seems to have no clear end, no guaranteed victory. Some days feel like I'm stuck in the past, replaying old wounds, old mistakes, old failures in my mind. It's easy to get lost in the memories of those dark seasons, believing that they define who I am or will always be a part of my story.

Embracing New Beginnings: A Divine Call to Move Forward

But then, I come across a verse like Isaiah 43:18-19 (NIV). "Forget the former things; do not dwell on the past. See, I am doing a new thing!" It's as though God is speaking directly to me, urging me to let go of what's behind and to look ahead to what He's doing right now. It's easy to get trapped in the past, especially when the weight of depression clouds our vision. We may hold onto memories of past failures, mistakes, or even past pain because it feels familiar. It's what we've known for so long. But God's word in Isaiah reminds us that he is continually working to do something new. He's not asking us to forget our experiences altogether, but to let go of the power they have over us. He's calling us to look up and see that He's moving, even when we feel stuck.

For me, depression often feels like being trapped in a dark tunnel, with no clear way out. I've struggled with the idea that this dark season will never end, that it will always be a part of who I am. But this verse speaks to the hope that God is working during the struggle, even when it feels impossible to see. He's making a way where there seems to be no way. He's doing a new thing, whether I see it or not.

Finding Hope and Growth in the Midst of Darkness

God doesn't promise that the darkness will vanish overnight. But he does promise that he's doing something new in us, through us, and for us. Depression might make it hard to see the light, but it doesn't mean the light isn't coming. Sometimes the "new thing" God is doing is not in the absence of darkness, but in how we grow and heal through it. God is with us in the valleys, even when we can't see how things are changing.

The past can have a hold on us, especially when it's filled with memories of pain, regret, or lost hope. But God's call is clear: we don't have to stay there. We don't have to let the past define us. He's doing a new thing in our lives. It might not be evident right away, but the promise is there. God is at work, bringing renewal, healing, and hope, even in the places where we feel the most broken.

Embracing Healing and Restoration Through Faith

If you're struggling with depression or any form of past hurt, remember that you don't have to dwell on the pain. God is not asking us to forget our experiences, but to trust that he is doing something new, something that will bring healing and restoration. It's okay if the road is long and difficult; the promise of a new thing is still there.

Prayer:

Lord, I bring my past and my struggles before you today. I've often found myself trapped in old hurts and memories, unable to see beyond the darkness. Please help me to forget the former things, to release the grip of the past, and to trust that you are doing a new thing in my life. Open my eyes to see your work in my present and my future. Even when the way feels unclear, please help me to rest in the hope that you are always at work, bringing healing and transformation. In Jesus' name, Amen.

Your Turn:

What is one step you can take today to shift your focus from the past and open yourself to the new things God is doing in your life?

Katherine Hutchinson-Hayes
This Bittersweet Season

He restores my soul. He leads me in paths of
righteousness for His name's sake.
Psalm 23:3 (ESV)

Restoration is a theme that has woven its way quietly, but determinedly, through the halls of our home. After years of laughter, tears, late-night conversations, and endless piles of laundry, my husband and I now find ourselves with just one child at home. The once-bustling bedrooms are quieter, echoing memories rather than the daily sounds of active children. We find ourselves, in many ways, standing in the ruins—not of something terrible, but simply of something once full, now made empty by life's natural progression.

Revitalizing Our Home and Partnership

In the midst of this bittersweet season, we are tackling home projects with newfound purpose. Walls are getting fresh coats of paint. Old posters are coming down. Spaces once dedicated to childhood pursuits are being repurposed, reimagined, and given tender attention. We laugh together as we assemble furniture or pull up carpet, exchanging stories along with paint rollers. There's a sense of reclaiming, not just the house, but also each other and our partnership, which—like the rooms themselves—is being refreshed and renewed.

The restoration is not just physical. With each project, God reminds me that He, too, is in the business of restoration. He allows us to walk through seasons—some bustling and some quiet—where we may feel a sense of loss but are given opportunities for renewal. Scripture is full of God's promises to restore what was lost: "He restores my soul. He leads me in paths of righteousness for His name's sake" (Psalm 23:3, ESV). Just as we make something new from what has become old or empty, God gently shifts, heals, and transforms us. He reclaims our hearts, renews our spirits, and gives us new purpose when seasons change.

Embracing the Sacred Transition to an Empty Nest

Yes, we miss the busy, noisy days. There are pangs of sadness as we watch our children step boldly into adulthood. But in this space—this new, quieter version of home—we are discovering joy, creativity, and renewed intimacy. God invites us to trust Him with our emotions and hopes. He promises to bring restoration not only to our physical spaces but to our very souls—reminding us that every season is sacred, and each transition is a new opportunity for growth and grace.

Prayer:

Lord, thank You for being the great Restorer. Help us to embrace every season, trusting You to renew what feels empty and to fill what aches with loss. Restore our hearts, our homes, and our relationships. Grant us joy as we discover new purposes and renewed hope in You. Amen.

Your Turn:

- How is God restoring you in this season?
- What areas of your life, home, or heart are being renewed?

Kathy Keenum
Caught Up in the Race:
Why We Miss What Matters Most

Do not be conformed to this age, but be transformed
by the renewing of your mind, so that you may discern
what is the good, pleasing, and perfect will of God.
Romans 12:2 (HCSB)

The Race for Worldly Pleasures: A Reflection on Modern Life's Distractions

I often watch people rush around, busy going here and there. I realize that their goals frequently revolve around pleasure, possessions, or status and power. I notice that worldly pleasures and desires seem to be their only guide. Sometimes, I feel caught up in the race too, like I'm a mouse scurrying everywhere—easily disturbed and distracted. I catch myself thinking that the only aim is to satisfy my needs, driven by instinct and desire. I see that the values of the world can easily become my guide as I get deeper into this mindset, ultimately leading me nowhere but into an endless cycle.

The world is full of attractions designed to fool us—telling me I must do this to be cool and accepted, that I have to do that to have friends, to do whatever feels good. I recognize these patterns in myself and wonder how often they influence me. I understand that the endless cycle of chasing the world and its idols causes me to miss what matters most—discerning what is the good, pleasing, and perfect will of God.

Transformed by Christ: Overcoming Worldly Temptations Through Faith

The distractions of the world are very tempting. But the world belongs to the evil one. He is the deceiver. The endless lure of desires, money, power, fame, and physical pleasures pulls us away. However, when we accept Christ, believing that He led a perfect life, died on the cross as payment for our sins, and then rose again three days later, we're transformed. Christ changes our lives and our attitude. Our mind and our heart are then changed. We become transformed by renewing our minds, focusing on Godly things, and leaving behind worldly views. It's doable but not always easy.

As we walk with Christ, we're more likely to remember to pray and study the Bible regularly. It's during our study time that we should pause, be still, and listen. During these moments, we may hear God speak to us through a feeling, a word, or a verse. If we open our minds to them and keep our eyes open, we may begin to recognize what the Lord is trying to tell us and discern His will.

Shaping Your Own Path: The Power of Intentional Living

Consider the idea that our life stories are often shaped by external influences, but we have the power to choose our own path. Instead of purely acting on impulse or fleeting desires, reflect on what truly guides us—whether it's our values, faith, or inner convictions. Strive to be the person you aspire to be, working toward meaningful goals and making a positive impact on others along the way.

Prayer:

Lord, I come to you today believing that Christ paid the cost for my sins by dying on the cross and rising on the third day to pay for my sins. Christ's sacrifice has afforded me the gift of eternal life. Please continually renew my spirit and guide me throughout my days, that I may make good choices and follow your will for my life. Allow me to be a good example to others. I praise you, the almighty King. You are our beginning and our end. We would be nothing without you. Amen.

Your Turn:

- Do you have a personal relationship with Jesus Christ?
- Has Christ transformed your attitude and behavior as you go about your daily life?
- Do you live your life in the world or centered on the Lord?
- Are you following the Lord's will for your life?
- Do you take time to listen to him each day?

Kelly Fordyce Martindale
Restoration May Tary But It's Never Late

Even if my father and mother abandon me, the Lord
will hold me close.
Psalm 27:10 (NLT)

Age twelve and the oldest of four, I gathered my siblings into a huddle to shield them. Our parents were pointing shotguns at each other in our living room. I thank God they didn't pull the triggers

Half a century later, both parents, long divorced, show end-of-life symptoms. Tears fall or laughter bursts without warning; the emotions are tumultuous.

We bury memories, regrets, and trauma. Each of us have suppressed our parents' behaviors and demons for over sixty years. Burdens no child should carry. With their deaths, will peace come, or grief and relief collide? The scars are deep.

There is love and honor, as God commands. But what of the emotions in between—anger, sorrow, disappointment, resentment, fear, and insecurity of never having been protected?

That twelve-year-old inner child still tries to shield everyone. Today I hold hospital paperwork and read texts instead of facing rifles, but the same helplessness lingers. Have I made the right decisions?

My siblings and I converse about DNR choice, burial and cremation. Is this the final deathbed goodbye? These practical talks carry the weight of a lifetime. We pray for wisdom.

My siblings and I process differently—one leans toward compassion, another stays distant; one handles medical decisions, another legal. Together we've woven a tapestry of perspectives, frayed at the edges, wrestling with death and decades of tangled emotions.

I've grappled with honor. When parents inflicted harm, does it mean pretending pain isn't real or offering unearned affection? No.

Maybe it means choosing dignity: showing respect for life, humanity, and acknowledging brokenness. I've chosen not to repay evil with harm or curse them. I will treat them as image-bearers of God, even if brokenness obscures that truth.

Thinking toward funerals, I'm remembering a few good memories, by God's grace. Once our parents left us in the woods at our turquoise GMC pickup. We found a pond and scrambled after huge hopping toads. We tossed frogs into the bed of the truck, so many, they covered the floor of the truck.

Those glimpses of grace don't erase the turmoil but are shafts of light cutting through the long nights of smashing coffee cups, screaming, and grunting. They remind me God's hand has been steady even when everything else shook. It's as if God Himself seemed to whisper, "You are mine. I see you. I will never leave you."

And He never has.

Forgiveness doesn't mean what happened was okay. It means refusing bitterness, handing over the justice I long for to the One who judges rightly. I no longer carrying the weight of fixing the unfixable.

Letting go means recognizing a true Father who never failed me or abandoned me to instability. When our parents pass, their brokenness won't have the final word. Our story is restored with the grace God gives us to extend to our own children and grandchildren. We have a legacy of faith to pass forward instead of repeating the past.

That's our redemption. God's writing a new story out of old pain, lifting the burden of a frightened twelve-year-old and giving me peace to share with my siblings. What was stolen in childhood is restored today and into eternity.

We cannot choose the families we're born into, but we can choose the legacy we leave. Honoring our parents doesn't erase harm, but reflects God's mercy, and forgiving frees us from bitterness.

Most of all, trusting God as our true Father heals what no earthly parent could. I find peace in the arms of the Lord, who never lets loose. In that truth, I breathe freely.

Prayer:

Lord Jesus, I praise you for knowing the hearts of each of us: what makes us the way we are and not leaving us like this. I don't want to live my elder years bitter and resentful. I surrender my pain to you. Please heal me fully. My mom is with you now, free of earth's sorrows. Thank you, Lord, for helping to trade the bitter for sweet as I said goodbye and I love you, and I meant it.

Your Turn:

- Have we received justice for the attacks we've experienced?
- Is there enough trust in our Creator to release those burdens and let the injustice go?
- Is there forgiveness?

- Individually, can we move forward into Christ's promised freedom?
- Will we choose the restoration only Christ offers?

Helena Smrcek
Restored to Wholeness

*He restores my soul; He leads me in paths of
righteousness for His name's sake.*
Psalm 23:3 (NKJV)

*Come to Me, all you who labor and are heavy laden,
and I will give you rest.*
Matthew 11:28 (NIV)

*The Lord will guide you always; He will satisfy your
needs in a sun-scorched land and will strengthen your
frame. You will be like a well-watered garden.*
Isaiah 58:11 (NIV)

We often mistake *self-care* for selfishness. Yet true self-care is not indulgence—it's restoration. It's how we make room for God to renew what life depletes. The pace of this world pushes us to fill every moment, but sometimes the most faithful act is to stop. When we pause long enough to breathe, pray, and listen, the Lord begins His quiet work of healing within us.

During difficult seasons—whether global upheaval or personal trial—it's tempting to slip into despair. Uncertainty, isolation, and endless bad news can fray even a steady heart. But Scripture calls us to guard our minds. Renewal doesn't begin with circumstance; it begins with surrender.

If you've ever looked at your day and thought, *I can't keep this up*, you're not alone. God never intended us to live on empty.

Jesus' invitation in Matthew 11 (NIV) isn't a poetic metaphor— it's a lifeline: "Come to Me... and I will give you rest." Real rest doesn't come from escape or distraction; it comes from leaning on Him.

Mind, Body, and Spirit

Caring for your body is an act of stewardship. Move, stretch, walk, or rake the leaves—whatever keeps your body alive. The ability to move is a gift, often taken for granted, until it gets taken away, in my case, by back pain.

Feed yourself well. Checking the nutritional labels on our food shouldn't be accidental. Make it a habit. Turn mealtime into a small liturgy of joy. Cook something wholesome, light a candle, and give thanks before each bite. Put the phone away. When we practice presence—even at the table—we rediscover contentment that no newsfeed can provide.

Your mind needs rest as well. Limit the noise that fuels anxiety. Step back from the constant scroll of headlines and lean into the timeless rhythm of Scripture. When you read a psalm or whisper a prayer, you're reminding your soul of what is unshaken. Faith doesn't deny hardship—it invites peace into it. Life is not about perfection or performance; it's about gratitude.

The Garden Within

In times of waiting, creation reminds us of God's rhythm. Plant something—even a small pot of herbs or a hardy succulent. Watch how life persists under the care of light and water. Tending the soil teaches us patience. Growth is invisible for a while, but that doesn't mean nothing's happening. The same is true of our spirit.

Old hobbies and forgotten joys are also seeds of restoration. Pick up the knitting needles, paintbrush, or journal. These quiet, creative acts untangle the mind, bring peace, and give shape to gratitude.

Restoring Connection

We're not meant to heal in isolation. Call a friend. Send a note. Offer kindness to your neighbor. Small gestures ripple wide in weary times. As Isaiah wrote, "You will be like a well-watered garden." Make this a regular part of your daily routine, and in no time you will notice your own restoration overflow—and refresh others too.

Prayer:

Dear Lord, please help me to guard my heart against false comfort. Please show me how to put away distractions that might numb the ache, but it won't heal it. Help me to see that true comfort is found in Christ's presence, in honest conversation, in laughter shared, in remembering that we belong to something eternal. Lord, restore my soul. Teach me to rest in You, to move with grace, and to reflect Your light to others. Amen.

Your Turn:

This season may feel like a long pause, but even pauses are holy if we let God inhabit them. Restoration isn't a return to who we were— it's a rebirth into who we're becoming under His care. Take time today to breathe deeply, read a verse aloud, and whisper a simple prayer.

Rachael M. Colby
Unconscionable Delay

Faith by itself, if it does not have works, is dead.
James 2:17 (NKJV)

Delay. Sometimes it's divinely ordained, but most times it's due to our negligence or obstinance. There are sins of commission (those we do) and sins of omission (when we fail to do as we ought).

Some delays are unconscionable. A heinous example of this is the slow enactment and delivery of the Emancipation Proclamation message that declared freedom for slaves in America.

Juneteenth, our new national holiday observed on June 19 that celebrates this freedom, was long overdue when finally signed into law on June 17, 2021.

Juneteenth commemorates Union General Gordon Granger reading General Order 3 in Galveston, Texas, on June 19, 1865, which informed people of the Emancipation Proclamation. However, that news came *two years after* the date Abraham Lincoln had declared it was to take effect (January 1, 1863), and two months after Confederate General Robert E. Lee surrendered his troops to Union General Ulysses S. Grant on April 9, 1865, at Appomattox, Virginia. That unconscionable delay was because the Emancipation Proclamation depended on the Union winning the Civil War and applied only to some states. Finally, the 13th Amendment abolished slavery for all in America in 1865.

June 19 became known as Juneteenth, otherwise called Emancipation Day or Freedom Day. Records show it as first celebrated in Texas on **June 19, 1866.** Nevertheless, many slave owners withheld that information even after the 13th Amendment passed. An unconscionable delay.

How heartbreaking that many African Americans taken captive and robbed of their rights continued to live as slaves though declared free, because delay denied them.

How tragic that they or anyone else is ever a victim of the evil of slavery, whether in the past or modern-day anywhere in the world. We must not turn a blind eye or deaf ear to oppression. Left unchecked, these sins spread like cancer.

Have we become complacent, content in ignorance, unaware of our history, and of others' needs today? Let us as Americans not settle for less than full victory or tolerate the hindrance of God-given unalienable rights and those granted in the Constitution of the United States.

Dr. Martin Luther King Jr. led the way with peaceful protest to bring about positive change during the Civil Rights Movement. He did not falter because the road was long, nor fall for the riotous snares of violence and hate, which lead to division, disaster, and death. May we as a nation carry on the cause, for there's more restoration work to be done. We become more effective at finding solutions if we inform ourselves before we form opinions. A good starting place is to pray for and listen to each other.

Do we heed when called to charge into battle with the banner of truth?

Today, there's a prevalent delay in declaring freedom from another type of slavery more dangerous than any, that not only cripples and destroys lives in every nation, but unless conquered, results in eternal death of the soul. The Bible calls it sin. This inherited condition of all humanity, our inborn nature, accounts for the sins we commit, whether in secret or openly.

"Jesus replied, 'I tell you the truth, everyone who sins is a slave of sin'" (John 8:34, NLT).

The good news is Jesus also said, "If the Son sets you free, you are truly free" (John 8:36, NLT).

Jesus is the ultimate freedom fighter. However, many have not heard the message. He paid the penalty for our sins over 2000 years ago at Calvary, securing freedom for all who repent of sin and accept Him as Savior.

Yet many today live as slaves to addictions, to past hurts, and in bondage to bitterness. Jesus offers salvation and adoption as sons and daughters of the King.

If we believe the Bible, why delay warning of the perils on the wide, destructive road that leads to Hell? How is it that sometimes those who live in the blessings of salvation hesitate to deliver Jesus' message of His gift to all? —Unconscionable delay.

Let's fight for righteousness and justice for all. And let us faithfully proclaim the ultimate freedom that Jesus offers: forgiveness, freedom from slavery to sin, restoration, and a right relationship with Him.

Don't delay.

Prayer:

Forgive me, Lord, for being silent when I should speak, for being slow to show others the way you paved to a restored life, an abundant life, and an eternal life. "Faith without works is dead" (James 2:17, NKJV). Lord, You said, "Go into all the world and preach the gospel to all creation" (Mark 16:15, NASB). May I rush to bandage the wounded with the balm of Your love, defend the innocent, and help establish justice and righteousness. Help me seek and speak the truth boldly in love. Thank you for the solution to sin: the forgiveness, salvation, and freedom to flourish that you offer all. In Jesus' name, I pray. Amen.

Your Turn:

God has not called us to comfort or convenience, but to the cross, to bear one another's burdens.

Rodney Combs
Within Spitting Distance

*Brothers and sisters, if someone is caught in a sin,
you who live by the Spirit should restore that person
gently.*
Galatians 6:1 (NIV)

We long for the day when God completes his restoration of the earth and our lives. But until then, we have regular opportunities to restore others.

I watched an old law show where a brash reporter sneered, "Why are we even going to trial. Just look at him. He's guilty as sin."

Granted, the suspect was a beast—angry, snarling, shackled in an orange jumpsuit. His scraggly, bearded face covered an oversized head that melted into his massive shoulders, each of which anchored arms with biceps bulging larger than most men's legs. The lawyers kept a table between him and them to keep from being devoured, but it couldn't shield his spit.

Nearly everyone had given up on him.

Except one lawyer.

She saw through the rage and saliva.

She noticed a wounded man whose fury came from pre-judgment and a tumultuous past. The attorney listened, became curious about his story, and offered hope. Almost instantly, the defendant's shoulders dropped and his face relaxed.

When we're caught in our mess, our brains launch into hyper-protective mode. We wrestle chains of guilt and disappointment.

We're slow to trust that anyone, especially God, still believes in us, let alone desires to help.

When we're the not-caught ones, we need that attorney's attitude and approach to restore others. People around us are desperate for restorative grace, just as the Galatians are.

Before Galatians 6:1, we read about the listeners in chapter 5. Paul charged them to "walk by the Spirit" and flee the "desires of the flesh." He even contrasted the fruit of a Spirit-attuned life and a fleshly one.

If tempted to focus our restoration only on those with "minor" mistakes, we'd benefit from reading Paul's list of depravities ugly enough to make our TV defendant look tame (5:19-21).

When we see people entangled in such sins, we're to "restore" them. The Greek word used in 6:1 is *katartizō*, which means "to put in order" or "to rebuild to its former condition."[7] The "former condition" refers to Christ-like character and conduct.

This restoration isn't to church membership.

It's more profound.

More gutsy.

Radical.

Life-infusing.

Paul charged those who "live by the Spirit" (not perfect people, but those training and gaining in the Christian way) to move within spitting distance and guide the other out of their sins to a healthier soul, identity, and character—to help them reorder their lives and rebuild themselves. But how?

Our TV lawyer shows the way, and so does the word "gently." "The work of restoration," writes New Testament scholar Timothy George, "should be done with sensitivity and consideration and with no hint of self-righteous superiority."[8]

Here's how that works:

1. *Don't pre-judge the person or the cause.*
2. *Stay curious.* Ask questions. Listen deeply.
3. *Offer empathy, not advice.* Help them explore their insides. Trust the Spirit's work.
4. *Cast the vision—the one about who they truly are, despite their mistakes.* Our behaviors flow from our needs. In low moments, we relish reminders that we're safe, valued, wanted, good enough, and called to a purpose. Sin loses its grip when God's love breaks through.
5. *Finally, ask who they want to become and how you can support them.* People own the process when they choose their own path. But no one wants to go alone.

Prayer:

God, our great Restorer, help us walk in your Spirit so that we can gently invite others to a rebuilt life. Amen.

Your Turn:

Before you look for someone else to restore, remodel your own life (Matthew 7:3-5). Then, in humility, find someone floundering. Don't pre-judge. Stay curious. Resist advice-giving. Cast vision. Ask how you can partner with them for beautiful restoration. If we do it right, their shoulders will drop, and hope will rise.

Sharmen Oswald
Worthy

*I praise you because I am fearfully and wonderfully
made; your works are wonderful,
I know that full well.
Psalm 139:14 (NIV)*

Our world and culture are consumed with images and messages instructing us to find our satisfaction, worth, and self-confidence in things. We are bombarded with ideology through social media, the news, and even family and friends telling us how to live our lives so that we feel good about ourselves. It is no wonder that depression and anxiety are at an all-time high. If you've ever been told that you are less than, not a good fit, or unworthy, you know how that can sting and hurt.

My faith was challenged when I was asked to overlook something that was immoral and wrong, even in the eyes of man and most certainly in the eyes of God. To make matters worse, the person who asked me to turn a blind eye was my supervisor. It took bold faith to stand up for what I knew was right and Godly, even if it would cost me my job. That is exactly what happened. My contract was not renewed to return and teach at the school where I had been teaching for 31 years.

When my supervisor called to deliver the news like a bomb, I asked why. He replied that I was no longer a good fit and that I did not have the right disposition. I was devastated and went immediately with my husband to my pastor to seek Godly counsel. We prayed together that I would have discernment and peace in the situation. For the rest of the school year, about three months, I packed up everything and prepared to leave what I had called home for thirty-one years. It wasn't easy to go there every day, knowing that I was not coming back. For the rest of the school year, I felt invisible and unseen. I dug deep in my soul to find faith to continue to believe that God was in charge and held me in the palm of his hand.

My worth as a teacher was challenged and damaged by hurtful, stinging words from someone who is supposed to encourage and build up. One morning as I prayed, God spoke to my heart, telling me that I was more worthy in His eyes than in the eyes of man. He drew me to His word, specifically to Philippians 1:6, which told me, "I am certain that God, who began the good work within you, will continue his work until it is finally finished on the day when Christ Jesus returns." That verse resonated with me, and I repeated it several times throughout the day. I heard the truth in it, that just because I was finished as a teacher God was not finished with me.

I began to see that I am precious in God's eyes because he created me in His image. "Then God said, 'Let us make man in our image, after our likeness" (Genesis 1:26, NKJV). God used this painful situation to draw me back to the understanding of my worth gifted through the sacrifice of His Son Jesus Christ. Other verses began to speak to my heart, becoming a healing balm for my soul. My demeanor became brighter and lighter knowing that I am worthy of God's love and that he accepts me just as I am. I asked His forgiveness for placing too much worth in man, in the world, and in my work. You see, my identity had been wrapped up in being a teacher rather than in being God's image bearer and Jesus' ambassador.

When I studied the Hebrew meanings of the words "worth" and "worthy," I was amazed at how one word could lead me to such profound Godly understanding. In Hebrew, worthy means "to be fit or appropriate" and can also mean "to be seen."[9] When I was told I was no longer a good fit, God thinks I am a good fit and appropriate. When I felt invisible, God saw me.

Prayer:

Father God, I lift up the person to you who is feeling unworthy, downtrodden, depressed, and anxious. Help them to see their worth in you, not in the world. Open their hearts to the truth that you love them unconditionally. Help them to know that You see them, that they are not invisible, and that they are precious to you. Draw them to your side and help them to abide in you. Shift their focus from the world and man to you. Strengthen their faith in You and hold them in the palm of Your hand. I pray this in the name of Jesus, Your Son. Amen.

Your Turn:

- Have you ever experienced rejection?
- Were there times when others made you feel as if you were unworthy?
- Have you struggled with feelings of not being enough?

Now is your time to correct those untrue feelings or words you or others spoke over your life. No matter what happens, remember that God's got you and you were made for more. More of His favor, more of His grace, more of freedom from depression, anxiety, and rejection.

Cecil Taylor
Always on Restoration Road

*Brothers and sisters, I do not consider myself yet to
have taken hold of it. But one thing I do: Forgetting
what is behind and straining toward what is ahead, I
press on toward the goal to win the prize for which
God has called me heavenward in Christ Jesus.
Philippians 3:13-14 (NIV)*

When a structure collapses, the event happens quickly. Further
analysis typically reveals the time and sequence of events required to
cause the collapse.

Our family was living what I thought was a normal life. In the next
moment, an ambulance was whisking my unresponsive wife, Sara, to
the hospital. Later, I was shocked to hear the overdose was intentional.
The next morning, the doctor instructed me to take Sara straight from
the medical hospital to a psychiatric hospital. Less than fifteen hours
after I called the ambulance, doors closed behind Sara as she, and
figuratively the entire family, entered a new world.

Our old life had collapsed into ruins.

Of course, I attempted to rebuild it all. I tried to return life to
normal for our three children, ages eleven and under. But there was no
normal to which we could return, no more than you could reassemble
the pieces of a crumbled building into the exact structure it was before.

The truth was, our old life was a lie. Sara had simply swallowed
her depression, dating back to her formative years, as long as she
could. Now we had to finally start living in the truth.

Living And Learning

One suicide attempt twenty-two years ago led to nine more attempts. Or ten; I've lost count. The new truth—the day-to-day living, not just the most dramatic moments—was so difficult, I think we've all blocked out portions of it.

Recently, reading through my journal entry from nine years after the worst day of our lives, I realized how close our marriage came to shattering. I remember how long it took me to find my footing, to learn how to be the best husband I could be for my depressed wife. While I tried various resources available to me, I'm not sure any held the exact answers. I had to learn for myself through trial and error.

Meanwhile, through medicine, counseling, and trusting herself and others, Sara gradually learned how she could fight her depression.

Accepting There's Never A Finish Line, Only A Journey

I want to say God delivered a miracle and took depression away from Sara. Such things can happen. Despite our prayers, her miracle never happened.

Or did it? Sara experienced a divine intervention at one point. The message was not that she would be healed. Instead, she would eventually tell her story. This piece is part of that storytelling.

Our journey doesn't have a finish line. Depression isn't like that. It lurks behind every happy face. It sneaks back into the room, uninvited, unnoticed. Depression can be triggered by the smallest of things, as one finds with grief. It can even arise from good times, the depressed person feels they don't deserve.

So, what does restoration look like when you're always on Restoration Road?

You develop vigilance, constantly looking for signs and signals, alert for relapse tendencies.

You find hope. Not the hope that we will solve the problem, but the hope you feel knowing you can carry each other. The hope that knows God is carrying all of us.

You find that love has a deeper meaning. You commit to living both in sickness and in health.

You reach acceptance. You accept the past, the present, and the future. You let go of the past and strain toward what lies ahead, believing the final restoration will take place in heaven, where tears are wiped away and our new bodies are perfect.

Prayer:

Lord, it's hard to realize that some broken pieces never get fixed. We lament the damage and cry out for your goodness and healing power. Please give us the strength to leave the ruins behind and to live each day as people traveling a road of restoration with you. Amen.

Your Turn:

- What are the broken pieces of your life that have never been fully repaired?
- How can you apply vigilance, hope, love, and acceptance to inform your journey toward restoration?

REFERENCES

1. Cambridge English Dictionary, 2024, Accessed 11/22/2025, https://dictionary.cambridge.org/us/dictionary/english/restore

2. TruelyRandomVerse, *Word Study for H1322—Strong's Definition,* Accessed 11/22/2025, https://trulyrandomverse.com/strongs/hebrew/1322

3. BibleHub, *Strong's Hebrew 4016*, Accessed 11/22/2025, https://biblehub.com/hebrew/4016.htm

4. World War II Fact Sheets, *The Historic D-Day Invasion: A Turning Point in World War II*, Chapel Hill, NC, Accessed 1/2/25, https://www.ibiblio.org/pha/pha/misc/World%20War%20II%20Fact%20Sheets.pdf

5. CBS Sunday Morning, *"The Wizard of Oz" as you've never seen it before*, https://www.youtube.com/watch?v=0gpwcaNyIrY

6. Dictionary.com, Accessed 11/22/2025, https://www.dictionary.com/browse/surrender

7. BibleHub. *Strong's Greek 2675*, Accessed 10/1/25, https://biblehub.com/greek/2675.htm

8. George, Timothy, *Leadership Lifts*, The Gospel Coalition, Accessed 10/1/25, https://www.thegospelcoalition.org/article/timothy-george-leadership-lifts

9. Pealim, *Pe'alím*, Accessed 9/9/25, https://www.pealim.com/dict/3955-rauy

ACKNOWLEDGMENTS

First and foremost, all glory and honor belong to God—the One who takes our broken places and turns them into testimonies of grace. Every devotion in these pages is evidence of His faithful hand, His restoring power, and His unwavering love. May this book point every reader back to Him, the Master Builder who never stops redeeming our stories.

I also want to honor the memory of my beloved parents and my brother, who are now with the Lord. Their lives were living examples of perseverance, prayer, and a faith that held fast in every season. They taught me—by word and by example—to keep drawing closer to God, to trust Him in the ruins, and to let Him make all things new. Their legacy continues to shape my calling, my heart, and my walk with Christ.

A heartfelt thank-you goes to the incredible contributors who poured their stories, wisdom, and faith into this devotional. Your vulnerability and courage will bless countless readers.

I would also like to extend deep gratitude to the entire Dressed in Love, LLC team. Your dedication, excellence, creativity, and heart for ministry made this project possible. To our Project Manager, editors, formatter, graphic artist, social media specialist, nonprofit consultant, technology expert, and legal support—you are the backbone of this work. Thank you for rising to every challenge, stewarding each story with care, and serving with such purpose and passion.

This book is a collective offering—a tapestry woven from many voices, many testimonies, and many hands. Thank you to everyone who believed in this project, prayed over its creation, and helped bring it into the world.

May God use these pages to restore hearts, renew hope, and remind us all that nothing in our lives is ever beyond His power to redeem.

In Christ,

Katherine Hutchinson-Hayes, Ed.D.

CONTRIBUTING AUTHORS

Vonyee Carrington lives in coastal Northeast Florida. She came to know the Lord Jesus Christ as a college senior. She is a woman who loves to help others find and follow their life's purpose. In her spare time, she enjoys reading, knitting, and writing. www.DrKatherineHayes.com/meetthebloggers

Rachael M. Colby has a heart for reconciliation and a passion to uplift those who serve in tough places. She writes to connect cultures' questions with Christianity's answers, inspire faith, and motivate. She's an award-winning writer in the categories of articles, poetry, devotions, essays, flash fiction, and children's picture books. Rachael is a freelance editor, a longtime member of The Jerry Jenkins Writers Guild, and a protégé in the Cecil Murphey Mentoring program. Her work has appeared in *Chicken Soup for the Soul*, "Blue Ridge Mountains Christian Writers Conference Blog", online publications, compilations, and the Oakridger newspaper. This Jamaican-born wife, mom, beach bum, artist, work in progress, resides in Cape Cod, Massachusetts. She runs on coffee, chocolate, and a whole lotta "Help me, Jesus," and blogs at: www.TattooItOnYourHeart.com.

Evelyn Collins lives in sun-drenched Florida with her husband, where they enjoy outdoor life most of the year. Before moving to the Sunshine State, Evelyn grew up near the ECU campus in North Carolina, with its sprawling, lush grounds of giant trees. She then moved to the Outer Banks with its lovely beaches, stunning sunrises, and sunsets. No matter where Evelyn lives, she finds solitude with God in nature, writing, and photography. The splendor of nature creates joy and wonder as it surrounds her, whether alone or among family and friends. In the summer of 2019, while strolling on the sandy shore of the Outer Banks, she stopped, snapped a picture, and picked up a comma-shaped shell. She felt God calling her to pause in God's presence, so she quickly recorded the beginning of a devotion on her phone. This was the beginning of her writing journey. As a photography enthusiast, she often uses her growing collection of photos as inspiration for her work. Evelyn also records inspirations from quiet time spent observing. Her writings express her deep appreciation of nature, God's presence, and gratitude for the many blessings enjoyed in life. www.EvelynCollinsAuthor.com

Rodney Combs, Ph.D., is an author, coach, and speaker. He is a Certified Primal Questions Coach. He uses his years of pastoring and leading to help others maximize their mission, serve and create, protect their souls, and find meaningful, unhurried fulfillment. The question behind his writing is, "How can we journey better with Jesus?" www.RodneyCombs.com

Andy Hollifield is a multi-award-winning author whose work has appeared on christiandevotions.us, cbn.com, and in three compilation books, *Room At the Table*, *Focus-45 Devotionals To Keep Jesus In The Picture*, and *Mountains Moved-45 Devotions On Bold Faith*. He is also the senior writer for "The Man Cave" on Dr. Katherine Hutchinson Hayes website. His first book, *Down Home Wisdom-Faith, Freedom, and the Front Porch Way of Life*, will be released on December 2, 2025, and has a Facebook page by that name. His second book, *Breaking Point-Stories to Keep You Going Volume 1*, is scheduled to be released in the summer of 2026. He is a former pastor, truck driver, and current missionary, having founded H.O.P.E. Ministries in 2002 to serve crisis agencies throughout Western North Carolina. He is currently working on *Breaking Point Volume Two*, and has plans for five more books, including novels, devotionals, and short stories. He posts daily on Facebook on weekdays and has a website at www.DownHome.media

Monica Hopper is intent on one thing—to know and see evermore the glory of God and to reflect Him through her thoughts, words, home, and family. Monica is a wife, mother of five, and a retired Navy senior chief. She currently homeschools three of her children. Monica has also done this while traveling the United States in an RV for almost a year. She holds a master's degree in leadership and management. www.DrKatherineHayes.com/meetthebloggers

Ken Howard has a keen eye for God's creative hand in nature has led him to capture inspirational images from behind his camera. As a professional photographer, his work in nature, wildlife, and human-interest photography has earned many awards from Iowa State University Extension in Marion County, as well as photo-related articles published in the local Pella Chronicle, Knoxville Journal-

Express, and Red Rock Lake News. When not behind a camera, Ken enjoys spending his time with his wife, Colleen, and their Labradoodle, Frankie. He also loves spending time in the Word, reading devotionals, hiking, backpacking, cycling, and playing bass for fun and on the church's worship team. KaleidoscopeImages.co

Colleen C. Howard is a Jesus follower, educator, and writer. She lives with her husband in the Arizona desert, where the sunsets are spectacular, the summers are relentless, and the winters are a little slice of heaven. Over the last few years, God has placed a strong desire in Colleen's heart to shine a light on God's presence throughout ordinary days and encourage women in their faith walk. Colleen's MA in Educational Leadership allowed her opportunities to write science curriculum, develop district programs, work with Arizona teachers, community leaders, and more. With NASA Grant funding, Colleen worked with teachers across the country, expanding their knowledge of teaching science as a collaborative effort. Online Publications: "Living By Design Ministries", "Her View From Home", "Insideout Worldwide", and "Inkspirations". Monthly Blogger at: "Dressing in God's Love" and "Devotionals for the Heart". Featured Anthologies in: *From Ruins to Restoration, Mountains Moved: 45 Devotions of Bold Faith, The Miracle of Prayer.*
www.facebook.com/gritgracecolleen, AuthorColleenCHoward.com

Katherine Hutchinson-Hayes, Ed.D., is a vibrant educator, speaker, author, and leader whose warmth and authenticity motivate others to live with bold faith and purpose. With more than twenty years of experience in leadership, supervision, and ministry, she has led initiatives in women's and children's programs, education, and organizational development. A talented storyteller and creative visionary, Dr. Katherine is an award-winning author and editor who previously served as Production Editor for Embolden Media Group. She is also the proud founder and owner of Dressed in Love Press, LLC, a traditional Christian publishing company dedicated to creating books that uplift, empower, and reflect God's truth. Her creativity extends beyond writing, as she hosts the award-winning podcast "Murder, Mystery & Mayhem Laced with Morality," which reaches listeners in over 66 countries worldwide. Through this platform, she explores storytelling that entertains while encouraging deeper reflection on justice, morality, and faith. Dr. Katherine's works include suspense fiction, devotionals, and Christian living—each infused with insight and spiritual depth. Known for her engaging speaking style and heart for people, she blends humor, vulnerability, and Scripture to inspire others to embrace their identity, purpose, and victory. An artist, pianist, and gourmet cook, she continues to live creatively and lead with compassion. www.DrKatherineHayes.com

Crystal Johnson (Minister) is a devoted mother, proud grandmother, and licensed minister with a heart for faith and family. As a widow, she has embraced life's challenges with grace and resilience, finding joy in the love of her three amazing daughters and her cherished grandson. Crystal is also a businesswoman, serving as one of the owners of T&E Seasonings, where she brings passion and dedication to her work. She holds an associate's degree in business administration, equipping her with the skills to thrive in entrepreneurship. In her spare time, she enjoys creating beautiful works of art through arts and crafts and making lasting memories with her grandson. She is the project manager for Dressed in Love Press. www.DrKatherineHayes.com/meetthebloggers

Shai Johnson is a dedicated paralegal at a law firm, bringing expertise backed by a bachelor's and master's degree in criminal justice, as well as a Paralegal certificate. With a passion for law and advocacy, she is committed to making a meaningful impact in the legal field. Beyond her professional work, Shai is an avid reader and writer who finds joy in storytelling. She is the author of the children's book *The Magical Butterfly*, captivating young minds with tales of wonder and imagination. https://www.drkatherinehayes.com/meetthebloggers

Kathy Keenum is an innovative freelance writer and published author. She worked for several years as a freelance journalist, then moved to technical and process writing. She served as an electronics technician in the United States Navy. While in the Navy, she met and married her husband, Ken. They raised two wonderful sons. Her love of writing outside of the work environment developed from a hobby to a second profession and winning her several awards at the Florida Christian Writers Conference.

www.DrKatherineHayes.com/meetthebloggers

Kelly Fordyce Martindale is a steady, trustworthy voice for anyone longing for hope, truth, and a reminder that God is still tenderly at work in our everyday lives. Those who know Kelly personally will tell you she writes exactly the way she lives—honest, compassionate, determined to wrestle with the hard things, and always searching for the heartbeat of God in the middle of real life. Her readers often say that Kelly has a way of putting into words what they've felt but couldn't quite articulate. Whether she's unpacking grief, telling a story from her own journey, or offering a gentle spiritual insight, she connects with people across generations—especially women walking through seasons of transition, loss, or renewal. Kelly's writing blends vulnerability, wisdom, and a touch of humor in a way that makes you feel like you're sitting across the table from a trusted friend. Her articles, books, and devotional reflections consistently point readers back to the comfort and strength found in Scripture. If you're looking for encouragement that meets you where you are, or a voice that feels both familiar and deeply grounded, you'll want to stay connected with Kelly's work. Sign up and journey with her—you'll be blessed by every word. She lives in Colorado with her husband of 35 years, close to her son and grand dog, and a bit too far away from her daughter and grandchildren. She's the only one who isn't a Colorado native but is transplanted from Idaho. www.KellyFordyceMartindaleAuthor.com

DiAnn Mills is a bestselling author who invites her readers to step into stories where suspense meets adventure and romance warms the heart. Known for crafting unforgettable characters tangled in unpredictable plots, DiAnn believes every breath we take unfolds a story waiting to be told—so why not make it thrilling? Her novels have consistently landed on bestseller lists including CBA, ECPA, and Publishers Weekly, and have won prestigious awards such as the Christy, Selah, Golden Scroll, Inspirational Readers' Choice, and Carol awards. DiAnn is a founding board member of American Christian Fiction Writers and Conference Advisor for the Blue Ridge Mountains Christian Writers. She actively participates in the Advanced Writers and Speakers Association, Mystery Writers of America, the Jerry Jenkins Writers Guild, and International Thriller Writers. DiAnn passionately invests in helping fellow authors succeed through mentoring, book coaching, and editing. She travels nationwide, speaking and teaching engaging writing workshops. A proud coffee snob who roasts her own beans, DiAnn also enjoys diving into good books, experimenting in the kitchen, and unabashedly spoiling her grandchildren—whom she insists are the smartest kids in the universe. She makes her home under the sunny skies of Houston, Texas. Connect with DiAnn online for behind-the-scenes glimpses, writing tips, and lively discussions: www.DiannMills.com

Terrance Niedziela Jr. grew up in Wisconsin and currently lives in South Carolina with his beautiful wife and their dogs. He received his BS in Ancient Middle East History with a minor in Creative Fiction at the University of Wisconsin-La Crosse and an MA in English and Creative Fiction Writing at Southern New Hampshire University. He currently teaches middle school English and writes speculative fiction. His fiction has earned a first-place Foundation Award at the Blue

Ridge Mountain Christian Writers Conference, a Fiction Carolina Christian Writers Award, and a second-place Florida Tapestry Award. His debut fantasy novel, *Becoming Fire & Lightning*, comes out Spring 2026. www.TerranceNiedzielaJr.com

Sharmen McAlister Oswald enjoys writing poetry and prose. She especially finds joy in pointing others to their God-given purpose while reminding them of God's promise for them. Having experienced several upheavals in her life, she prefers to look at these events as a proving ground for exercising and growing her faith. Sharmen is the leader of Pegasus Poets and a member of Foothills Writers Guild, both based in Anderson, South Carolina. She and her husband of 38 years are almost finished raising their children, as their son is a college senior and their daughter is an elementary teacher. Presently, Sharmen is a school Librarian and loves teaching. Her background in education includes English at the high school and middle school levels and math and science at the elementary level. She holds three degrees: a bachelor's in English, a master's in Library Science, and a specialist in Library Science with an emphasis in Administration. When not writing, Sharmen enjoys growing flowers. www.facebook.com/sharmen.oswald

Lilka Finley Raphael, A Florida native, has been a licensed pharmacist for over thirty years. Still, she has learned that the most potent prescriptions are not in bottles. Prayer and persistence are far more effective than any medication dispensed. A love for writing prompted Lilka to share her experiences and life lessons on her blogs

God, autism & me, B is for Blessed, and God and the Garden. Her latest endeavor, *Planted with Purpose, Devotions for Every Season*, explores God's wisdom as revealed in nature. This devotional challenges each of us to relinquish our personal preferences to God's greater purpose. Most recently, Lilka was fortunate once again to contribute to the Christmas edition of Refresh Magazine. Additional achievements for 2023 include contributions to Christiandevotions.us and "The Write Conversation". Lilka's entry, Broken Things, was recognized in the 2023 Advance His Kingdom Devotional Contest. Lilka's greatest achievements are her two adult sons who have flown the nest. Happily married for thirty-one years, she lives east of Atlanta with her husband, Rod. They now share their home with two German Shepherds—Holly and Ivy—and one naughty kitty, Moxie. www.LilkaRaphael.com

Helena Smrcek was fascinated by writing from an early age. In high school, she faced unwanted attention from the Czechoslovakian Secret Police for her writing. Four years later, still in high school but in the US, she was a refugee struggling with English. Yet, she managed to get her first three articles published in The Mississauga News. In 1999, Helena wrote a string of one hundred articles. She also had the opportunity to work in television production and met influential authors who mentored and inspired her. In October 2011, She published *Kingdom Beyond Borders*, a collection of true refugee stories. She's spent fifteen years developing her storytelling skills and hope her stories deliver style, substance, and unforgettable characters. www.HelenaSmrcek.com

Cecil Taylor founded CecilTaylorMinistries.com to teach Christians how to live a seven-day practical faith. In the four years since entering his ministry full-time, Cecil has authored four award-winning books, contributed to nine anthology books, and developed seven video studies for churches and small groups. Cecil writes the "Seven-Day Practical Faith" blog and hosts the Practical Faith Academy podcast. He operates a connected ministry to families through UnisonParenting.com. A lifelong Texan based in the Dallas area, Cecil has been married 40 years, with three adult children. He enjoys sports (especially the Texas Longhorns), music, travel, and gardening. www.CecilTaylorMinistries.com